No More Spectators

No More Spectators

*The 8 Life-Changing Values
of Disciple Makers*

Mark Nysewander

Sovereign World

Sovereign World Ltd
PO Box 784
Ellel
Lancaster LA1 9DA
England
www.sovereignworld.com

ISBN 978 1 85240 543 4

The publishers aim to produce books which will help to extend and build up the Kingdom of God. We do not necessarily agree with every view expressed by the author, or with every interpretation of Scripture expressed. We expect each reader to make his/her judgment in the light of their own understanding of God's Word and in an attitude of Christian love and fellowship.

Cover design by ThirteenFour Design
Typeset by CRB Associates, Potterhanworth, Lincolnshire
Printed in the United States of America

Dedicated to the memory of Phillip Karr.
He made disciples who are still making disciples.

*"If anyone would come after me,
he must deny himself and take up his cross daily
and follow me."*
(Luke 9:23)

Contents

Acknowledgements

The title for this book, *No More Spectators*, came from a mission statement. It was for Bethany Missionary Church in Bloomington, Minnesota. I am indebted to Kent Garborg, Matt Hedrick, Tom Lundquist and John Anderson for their willingness to listen to the Spirit together and begin a journey that is bigger than a church's mission statement. Our time in exploring relational Christianity helped me discover these kingdom values that give direction to disciple-making.

I am also indebted to Dr Robert Coleman and his classic work *The Master Plan of Evangelism*. In his little volume the eight values of Jesus' discipleship are clearly spelled out. I have based the values of a disciple-maker on the clear presentation of Dr Coleman's work. I have changed the sequence of some values and expanded the definition of others. I also put them in an alphabetical alliteration so they can be easily remembered.

Special thanks to my wife, Kathy, and colleague, David Eldridge, for making corrections and helpful suggestions to the manuscript.

Foreword

No More Spectators is a fresh statement of an ancient theme – reproducing the life and mission of Jesus in others. It is written with passion, authority and clarity.

While the teachings of Jesus convey a message of truth for the whole world, equally important are the relationships Jesus had with His followers. They model a method of ministry as vital as the message He taught. We cannot separate the life of Jesus from His teachings, just as we cannot separate the incarnation from the cross. All those who want to know and love Jesus intimately, must eventually imitate the way He lived, not just study what He taught.

The kingdom of God is advanced through knowing Jesus and leading others to know Him. There is no higher calling on this planet. It is a calling that belongs to every follower of Jesus Christ. No matter what your gift, no matter what your personality, no matter what your position, the words of Jesus to His disciples are the same words that He speaks to you and me today: "As you are going, teaching and baptizing – make disciples!" (Matthew 28:19–20).

Mark Nysewander has grasped the very heart of Jesus' ministry and summarized it for us in the pages in this book. I commend it and pray it will inspire you to have many spiritual sons and daughters.

Floyd McClung
International Director, All Nations
www.allnationstraining.com

Introduction

"If you want to build a ship, don't drum up men to go to
the forest to gather wood, saw it, and nail the planks
together. Instead, teach them the desire for the sea."

(Antoine de Saint-Exupéry)[1]

Desire for the Sea

There is an expression of the Church that is absolutely
stunning in its power to transform not just people but entire
communities. In multiplying waves of growth it breaks up
age-old demonic strongholds and releases revival. This vast
manifestation of Christianity knows no barriers. In history it
covered continents and renewed the work of Jesus Christ in
His people. Today it is the dominant form of church life, as
great and dramatic as the ocean.

Unfortunately, the contemporary Western Church has
rarely seen this active sea of grace. We have been in the sterile
desert of spectator Christianity. We dress up our anemic
churches with programs, entertaining events and fascinating
facilities but we don't make disciples who make disciples.
Many of us are not even aware of the relentless incoming tide
of relational Christianity that advances over Asia, Africa and
Latin America.

Brother Yun, one of the leaders in a Chinese house church
network that contains at least 58 million believers, speaks a
prophetic word to the Western Church. He declares, "When I

am in the West I see all the mighty church buildings and all the expensive equipment, plush carpets and state-of-the-art sound systems. I can assure the Western church with absolute certainty that you don't need any more church buildings. Church buildings will never bring the revival you seek. The pursuit of more possessions will never bring revival."[2]

Look beyond church the way we know it. View the majestic yet simple power of relational Christianity. When you do, you will desire for it. This is what we are made for as believers in Jesus Christ. How can we get to this ocean of life which is God's destiny for His Church?

Values over Models

You don't get to relational Christianity by drumming up believers to produce a new church model. For that reason this book is foremost about values instead of models. Embrace these discipleship values and you will get a desire for the sea. You'll know where you want to go. With the desire these values bring, you can find creative ways to get there embracing both difficulties and surprises on the way to disciple-making Christianity.

Please understand, there is nothing wrong with discipleship models. Right now there is a rich discussion in the Church about cells, house churches and other forms of relational Christianity. These strategies can be helpful in seeing why disciple-making Christianity works. But in the long run it is just as important to know why it is right as why it works. You can give yourself to what works for wrong reasons. Do a discipleship model without a passion for relational Christianity and any model can be hijacked by spectator Christianity for lesser purposes.

Not only that, there are people in spectator churches who cannot experience a cell church, house church or discipleship ministry. You may be one of them. You can still incorporate these values even if you belong to a spectator church. One of my first experiences of a genuine disciple-maker was a friend named Phillip Karr. He lived in the center of a spectator church but he passionately made disciples who are still making disciples.

As these values become embedded in your life and you do the work of disciple-making you will see relational Christianity. If you are in a cell church, house church or discipleship ministry these values will explain and enhance what you are doing. If you are in a spectator church these values will open the door to a Christianity you've longed to explore.

A Cry for Liberation

The title *No More Spectators* is not a finger-pointing judgment against a group of people who do church wrong. Nor is it meant to be a sign hung over the door of your church to keep certain people out. This is a cry of liberation!

We have all been spectators and it is time to explore the awesome high seas of disciple-making. Jesus is calling us to step into the dynamic, multiplying life of relational Christianity. The Western Church loves a private expression of faith. So the journey into community life will not be easy for any of us. But the same Holy Spirit who led the children of Israel out of the wilderness wanderings can lead us out of radical individualism into the values of a disciple-maker.

Come. Join the expedition. There are many surprises and dangers along the way, but the journey is exhilarating.

Notes

1. Quoted by Heike Bruch and Samantra Ghoshal in "Beware the Busy Manager," *Harvard Business Review* (Feb. 2000), p. 69.
2. Brother Yun with Paul Hathaway, *The Heavenly Man* (London: Monarch Books, 2002), p. 296.

Chapter 1

Don't Just Sit There

"The kingdom of God does not come with your careful observation."   (Luke 17:20)

"Do not merely listen to the word, and so deceive yourselves."
(James 1:22)

"You're a spectator. A passive listener. A blip."
(James H. Rutz)[1]

Running on All Cylinders

There are two ways to live out the Christian faith. Do it as a spectator or do it as a disciple-maker. If you choose to be a spectator you are not a heretic. Being a spectator has nothing to do with unacceptable theology. There are many strong, Bible-believing Christians who are spectators.

Being a spectator does not mean you are bad or more of a sinner than a disciple-maker. Again, there have been many deeply spiritual persons who have lived out their Christian life as spectators.

Nor will you find fanatical spectators who burn disciple-makers at the stake. Spectators admire and will even embrace some of the dynamics of a disciple-maker. Spectators generally don't launch inquisitions against disciple-makers.

So if spectators are not bad, wrong, or totally against disciple-makers, what is the problem with being a spectator?

If you can be a spectator and still come out OK in your Christian experience, why change? The issue is not how well you can do as a spectator. The issue is how much you will miss if you are not a disciple-maker. Spectator Christianity has been fine-tuned and well oiled over the years to produce the best possible spectator Christians. The best spectator, however, will never experience the fullness of what Jesus intended for us when He called us to be His disciples.

Not only that, many of the problems that are surfacing in the Western Church today come from the fact that spectator Christianity, the dominate cultural expression of the Christian life, is not working. James H. Rutz says, "All the major problems of the church today – other than sin – can be traced back 1700 years, to when the church became an audience."[2] In the West we have taken this audience paradigm to new levels of success as well as problems.

When Jesus was on this earth He gave His disciples a message and an experience of the kingdom. He also gave them a way to live it out. Today the Church is trying to live out the message and experience of the gospel in a way Jesus never intended. That is where the frustration comes.

Look at history. When you discover the church running on all cylinders you see a disciple-making church. Find the church misfiring and you've uncovered spectator Christianity. Oh, this kind of church still runs, but never at the spiritual velocity for which it was built. That's because God saved us to be a fellowship of disciple-makers not an audience of spectators. What are the differences between these two expressions of Christian life?

The Nature of Church

Spectators and disciple-makers have two different views of church. Church for a spectator is a passive experience. Spectators come to church to watch and listen. Hence they are spectators. Being passive doesn't mean spectators are not engaging with the information that is being taught or preached. They listen, watch and think. They can even go home and practice.

The arrangement of seating in the average Western church gives it away. This is the place for the primary meeting of believers. It is built for a group of people to come in, sit and watch what is going on in front. Church is a spectator experience. There is nothing wrong with this as an element in your Christian life, but for a spectator it is the primary way church is experienced.

To say spectators are passive does not mean they are inactive. They can be very active in their passivity. They busily go to many meetings, Bible studies, conferences and services. Spectator churches are notorious for filling calendars with activities every night, but the majority of these gatherings are passive. It is basically a time to come, sit and receive.

Christian Smith sums up this kind of believer quite well when he says, "Rather than contributing their part to edify the church, they go to church as passive receivers to be edified. Rather than actively spending the time and energy to exercise their gift for the good of the Body, they sit back and let the pastor run the show."[3] Spectators often choose a church because it makes no demands other than to come in once a week, sit and listen.

Church for disciple-makers is not passive. It is interactive. Their church life is marked by relational investment in other believers. They choose relationship over programs. They value one another over services and meetings. Their primary commitment is to relational Christianity where they interact with fellow believers.

This is not to suggest that a disciple-maker will never go to a service or Bible study. Acts 2:46–47 gives a snapshot of the early Church. It says,

"Every day they continued to meet together in the temple courts. They broke bread in their homes and ate together with glad and sincere hearts, praising God and enjoying the favor of all the people . . . "

These early disciple-makers attended the large gatherings but the interactive home meetings were primary.

John Wesley, the great disciple-maker of England, had large meetings but he made sure people came together in small interactive gatherings called classes. Wesley saw greater benefit in these interactive groups than in the passive meetings. He explained, "I have found by experience that one of these [believers] has learned more from one hour's close discourse than ten year's public preaching!"[4]

What happened in both those first-century Palestinian homes and eighteenth-century English homes? Hebrews 10:24–25 gives us a clue. It says,

> *"And let us consider how we may spur one another on towards love and good deeds. Let us not give up meeting together, as some are in the habit of doing, but let us encourage one another – and all the more as you see the Day approaching."*

The primary characteristic of church life for a disciple-maker is interaction with others. The primary characteristic of church life for a spectator is passive listening, watching and receiving.

The Nature of Discipleship

These two groups also differ in their view of discipleship. In spectator Christianity discipleship is personal. It is the follow-up for an individual who has just come to Christ. Sometimes discipleship is training in the Word to mature a believer. Because there is a great attrition in spectator churches, discipleship is also a relational web to keep a person from going out the back door of the church. In each of these situations discipleship is personal. It maintains a new convert, matures a believer or holds a church member through discipleship groups. All of these personal benefits are legitimate. But is personal benefit the ceiling for discipleship?

To the disciple-maker discipleship is not primarily a personal experience. It is a kingdom experience. You are a disciple of Jesus not simply to follow up a decision, gain knowledge or stay connected to a church. You are a disciple for kingdom breakthrough. Mortimer Arias is correct when he says, "Discipleship is in itself anticipation of the kingdom."[5]

In Mark 14:62 Jesus claimed He was the one who would bring the kingdom of God out of heaven at the end of history to transform the heavens and the earth. But Jesus also taught that before the end of history He would usher a measure of the kingdom into the world. It isn't the apocalyptic fullness that is yet to come. Rather He announced in Mark 1:14–15 a present sampling of the kingdom. From where would Jesus manifest this present in-breaking of God's power and presence?

Luke 17:20–21 gives us the answer:

> *"Once, having been asked by the Pharisees when the kingdom of God would come, Jesus replied, 'The kingdom of God does not come with your careful observation, nor will people say, "Here it is," or "There it is," because the kingdom of God is among you.'"*

Who was among the Pharisees as Jesus was speaking? Jesus was, but so also were His disciples. From where would Jesus bring this present in-breaking of the kingdom? He would bring it through Himself and His disciples.

Later in Matthew 16:19 Jesus said to this fellowship of disciples, *"I will give you the keys of the kingdom of heaven."* A new measure of God's presence and power is coming into the world through Jesus' disciples. Jesus reinvented discipleship. It existed before Jesus' day as the way a teacher taught his students. But Jesus made discipleship something entirely different. He made it a community of His followers through which He could now bring the kingdom of God into the world.

James Kallas, speaking of the ministry of Jesus with His disciples, explains, "Thus, in the demon-controlled world there were small islands. There were small places where the power of God recreating the world was already manifest. In this sense and only in this sense could the kingdom of God be considered present."[6] The kingdom comes in a localized expression through "islands" of Jesus' disciples.

Discipleship releases the power of God among the people of God. It is also the way God's presence breaks into a setting. God's reign in a community can be established through the disciples of the kingdom. While discipleship in spectator Christianity is mainly for personal needs, in relational Christianity it manifests a supernatural eruption of God's kingdom.

The Nature of Faith

Faith is also seen from two different perspectives. To the spectator faith is private. Faith is between the spectator and the Lord. No one else need be involved in the faith life of a spectator. Spectator Christianity is religious individualism. Although the church is here as a possible help to individuals, in the long run it is up to each individual to maintain his or her faith.

For some spectators faith is so private that it is possible to live the Christian life without the church. At times it seems to them easier to avoid the hassle of church life and simply be on the periphery or not participate at all. This doesn't affect the faith of a spectator because faith is private. This individualism makes church life at best optional and at worst non-existent.

Disciple-makers strongly disagree. Their faith began with an individual decision but after that it is corporate. Disciple-makers are not just saved from sin, they are saved into a community of believers to live out the full implications of their salvation. They cannot imagine a life of faith without others. The greatest blessings of the kingdom come in the corporate setting. In the New Testament there are at least forty-five "one another" passages that speak of the corporate nature of faith in Jesus. The major New Testament letters are addressed to the community of faith not to individuals. This doesn't mean you can't live your faith by yourself, but why would you?

Frank Viola explains, "The church, therefore, is not a collection of isolated Christian units meeting together as a congregation. Never! The church is a company of Christ-indwelt men and women who are being formed together by the power of the Holy Spirit. The church cannot be measured by individual units alone, for it is a corporate life – a collective spiritual organism."[7]

If you have never experienced the "collective spiritual organism" you may think that your individual faith is enough. It isn't. You are made to live out your faith in the richness of life together with other believers. Disciple-makers see the fullest measure of faith with one another.

God Is Not a Spectator

Once I was in a conversation with a fellow believer who was leaving our church because of our call no longer to be spectators. After some discussion he looked at me and said, "You don't understand. I want to be a spectator. This is where I want to stay." The expedition into relational Christianity is not easy. It demands death to values you have grown to enjoy and have incorporated into your Christian life.

But here's the good news. You can be changed. The life of God can transform you. Do you know why His life can change you? Because God is not a spectator. He is fully involved in you. Welcome the life of God through the Holy Spirit. Echoing in your spirit you will hear His cry of liberation, "No more spectators!" He will empower you to choose against your personal, individual and private choices for the purposes of the kingdom. It takes grace to be a disciple-maker but there is abundant grace for the journey.

Notes

1. James H. Rutz, *The Open Church* (Auburn: The Seed Sowers, 1992), p. 10.
2. Ibid., p. 11.
3. Frank A. Viola, *Rethinking the Wineskins* (Brandon: Present Testimony Ministry, 1998), p. 162.

4. Peter Burton, *Cell Groups and House Churches* (Ephrata: House to House Publications, 2001), p. 65.

5. Mortimer Arias, *Announcing the Reign of God* (Lima: Academic Renewal Press, 2001), p. 104.

6. James Kallas, *The Significance of the Synoptic Miracles* (Greenwich: The Press, 1961), p. 75.

7. Viola, *Rethinking the Wineskins*, p. 122.

Chapter 2

Aim for a Few

"He called his disciples to him and chose twelve of them ... "
(Luke 6:13)

"Greet also the church that meets at their house."
(Romans 16:5)

"The Church must be smaller before it can be substantially stronger." (Elton Trueblood)[1]

Not Any Gathering Will Do

There is more than one way to be a community of believers. Communities come in all sizes. You can join a large event with thousands or belong to a small group of a dozen or less. Not all gatherings, though, produce the same results. Each size meets a different need. Which community is the primary environment for making disciples?

Spectators value large gatherings. They aim for events. Spectators like these events full and interesting. If you are going to be passive and watch one event after another all your Christian life, you want those events to be good. Spectators define their primary community as the event they attend, whether it is a worship service, a class or a conference. A good spectator aims for the event.

Events are not the primary community for disciple-makers. They aim for a few. Jesus, the great disciple-maker, showed the primary gathering for kingdom breakthrough is a few people. He refused to aim for the event. He focused on twelve men and poured into them. Certainly there were big gatherings in Jesus' ministry. He fed the crowds several times. The teaching events in Capernaum were so big that people spilled out of the house. A large crowd gathered for the Sermon on the Mount. He did do events but He didn't *aim* for them. As a disciple-maker He gave Himself primarily to a few.

In fact, Jesus was so committed to a few that He told the people He healed not to tell others. He didn't want an act of compassion to become a healing event. When He was in Capernaum the whole town was looking for Him. He and the Twelve left the impressive crowd to go into small towns. Jesus wanted time with the few. He and His disciples would escape in boats, go off on secret retreats and hide away in homes. Being with a few was more important than being at a large gathering. Jesus understood that the primary gathering for the kingdom was not in a big event.[2] He aimed for a few because it produced high-octane community. Community is the environment where the kingdom flourishes. A disciple-maker always has a base community of a few.

The Place of Greatest Transformation

Give yourself to a few and it brings greater transformation to everyone's life. Why? The more concentrated your ministry, the greater the individual transformation. If you gather fifty bottles together and pour a pitcher of water over them some water will splash into the bottles. Now take one bottle. Carefully pour the water into it. You get much more water in that bottle. Concentrate the outpouring and more gets in the bottle.

At an event the outpouring of grace is diffused over many people. Although some measure of grace is imparted, it is not as great as when you minister in a concentrated community. When grace flows in a community of a few it fills and transforms.

However, there is one exception to this principle: revival. A revival is when a large gathering of people is radically transformed. So why is there such transformation in a revival event? Because the amount of grace being poured out is so much greater. Put those fifty bottles under Niagara Falls and they will get filled up (and knocked over and spun around). In revival the concentration of grace is in the outpouring instead of the community.

But the intense outpouring of revival won't last forever. These powerful manifestations of the Holy Spirit last for a season. Even though a revival event lasts for a period of time, revival transformation can continue and expand if you aim for a few. John Wesley saw something rarely seen in church history. He witnessed a revival that continued for over fifty years. George Whitefield, a contemporary of Wesley, confessed his own revival work dissolved like a "rope of sand" compared to what Wesley was doing. Wesley didn't draw more people to the event or preach any better than Whitefield. Yet Wesley was more successful in getting his people in small groups that became communities of kingdom power. The revival was transferred and preserved as people aimed for a few. Groups of a few provide a far more effective environment where lives can be transformed than do events attended by many.

Wesley's model came straight from Jesus. Jesus gathered around Him a few who saw kingdom breakthrough in their life together. Mortimer Arias, describing the power of this gathering of the few, says, "They were living manifestations of the new life in the coming kingdom, not only as individuals but also as an integrated group in their life and witness: a base community committed to Jesus and His kingdom."[3] They were a base community of disciples gathered around Jesus. The gathering for this kind of kingdom transformation is not the event but the community of a few. Out of concentrated relationship God's grace comes in strong doses. The primary community of a disciple-maker is always a few.

Where Love Shows Up

Love's strongest expression comes when you aim for a few. That is because love reaches its full intensity on the tracks of intimate community with a few others and with Jesus. Jesus promised in Matthew 18:20 that, when two or three are gathered in His name, He would be with them. He spoke of community. The two or three are not His minimal requirement for community. This number holds the strongest potential for His manifest presence of love.

Gather with a few to know both the love of Jesus and the love of the body. Remember Hebrews 10:24–25 which urges us to spur one another on toward love and good deeds. How can you do that in an event with hundreds of spectators sitting in pews and facing in the same direction? If love in the New Testament means patience, humility, tolerance and kindness, then you need to meet together in close community to live those dynamics out. Aim for a few and provide the primary environment for manifest love.

From a Few to an Event

But there is a problem. Christian community is a powerful expression of love. People who are starved for such an experience want to join the few. The more people that come into your small group, the bigger the group becomes until intimacy is finally lost. What once was a few now becomes many. And what once was a community now is an event. Manifest love begins to diminish.

Wolfgang Simson explains, "There is, in each culture, a very important numerical line between the organic and the organized, the informal and the formal, the spontaneous and the liturgical. I call this the 20-barrier, because in many cultures 20 is a maximum number where people still feel 'family,' organic and informal, without the need to get formal or organized."[4] Aiming for a few produces an environment where love is known in an informal community.

The success of aiming for a few can become its own worst enemy. The manifest love of Jesus draws more and more people until you no longer have a few. Do you refuse to grow in order to protect the loving community of a few? Some churches are so afraid of losing their family atmosphere that they keep people out. But the answer is not keeping people out. The answer is multiplying communities of love. Aim for a few. When people come, make more small gatherings of a few. The best way to grow in both love and numbers is to keep aiming for a few. When your group grows beyond a few, start a new group.

Expanding the Kingdom

Finally, aiming for a few expands the kingdom. Only when you aim for a few can you develop strong disciples who win the lost, protect new converts and multiply. I'm not suggesting you can't win many people to the Lord at an event. But event evangelism must be coupled with aiming for a few. Otherwise the majority of the people won at an event will never become disciples. Even with a strategic follow-up, out of 10,000 seekers in a large evangelistic event only about 100 will end up incorporated into the local church.[5] That is a one per cent retention rate!

Jesus won many people at large gatherings but He gave Himself to raise up and train twelve disciples. At the end of His ministry Paul said Jesus appeared to five hundred people (see 1 Corinthians 15:6). Out of that crowd of five hundred, only one hundred and twenty came to Jerusalem to wait for the outpouring of the Holy Spirit at Pentecost. That is ten believers for every one disciple that Jesus trained! Three years of ministry and all Jesus had to show for it was twelve men who could aim for a few in Jerusalem.

But a little more than a month after Jesus left the few, three thousand people were added to the Church. These one hundred and twenty got busy and started aiming for a few taken from the three thousand. They met in homes with a few and then gathered at large events for worship and teaching.

In Jerusalem the Church meeting in homes continued to grow. It reached between 10,000 and 15,000. After 250 AD the number of believers exploded into the millions. Growing at this rate, in three hundred more years Christianity would have spread from Turkey to the ends of the earth. But it began to slow down and stall out in growth. What happened?

Up to 300 AD archeologists can find no evidence for church buildings. All they can find are houses with Christian drawings on the wall. That's important. Buildings represent large gatherings. Homes represent small gatherings. Church life during the season of its greatest expansion was centered on aiming for a few. The average size of a church in a home was around twenty believers or less. After 300 AD the evidence of church buildings starts showing up. Events became the primary gathering of the Church. The momentum of conversion slowed down as the Church opted out of making disciples for spectator Christianity.

Expansion One House at a Time

Sometimes the Church gets back to aiming for a few as a result of the difficult changes of history. In 1982 the Communists in Ethiopia seized church buildings and imprisoned church leaders throughout the nation. Without buildings or professional pastors there were no more large public gatherings. The Meserete Kristos Church went underground and started meeting in homes with just a few believers in each home. This meant no more spectators. During the time of the Communist takeover the Church was forced into the value of aiming for a few. When Communism fell and the Meserete Kristos Church reemerged from its underground life, the Church had exploded from 5,000 believers to 50,000 within ten years, a tenfold increase.[6] Aim for a few and you will disciple many. The way to kingdom expansion is through the community of a few. It's the only plan of Jesus.

The primary community for a disciple-maker is a few. Howard Snyder reminds us that this has been true throughout church history and remains true today. Describing the house church which is one way to aim for a few, he says, "House churches have probably been the most common form of Christian social organization in all church history ... despite what we might think if we simply look around us here, hundreds of thousands of Christian house churches exist today ... In some sense, they are the underground church, and as such, represent the hidden stream of church history. Although they are hidden, and in most places not the culturally dominant form, these house churches probably represent the largest number of Christians worldwide."[7] Don't let the "cultural dominant forms" of gatherings deceive you from seeing the primary form of the kingdom. Aim for a few.

Notes

1. Quoted in *The Second Reformation* by William A. Beckham (Houston: Touch Ministries, 1995).
2. Robert Coleman, *The Master Plan of Evangelism* (Grand Rapids: Fleming H. Revell, 1963), pp. 33–35.
3. Mortimer Arias, *Announcing the Reign of God* (Lima: Academic Renewal Press, 2001), p. 6.
4. Wolfgang Simson, *Houses that Change the World* (Waynesboro: OM Publishing, 1989), p. 17.
5. Ibid., p. 280.
6. Ibid., p. 170.
7. Frank Viola, *Rethinking the Wineskins* (Brandon: Present Testimony Ministry, 1998), p. 55.

Chapter 3

Be with Them

"He appointed twelve ... that they might be with him ..."
(Mark 3:14)

"Let us not give up meeting together ..." (Hebrews 10:25)

"Discipleship is about people getting involved with each other." (Wolfgang Simson) [1]

Membership or Friendship?

Relationship is essential to making disciples. Since there are many ways to be with other people, what is the primary relationship for disciple-making? To spectators the basic relational connection they have with others is membership. Membership is a casual association. Simply join a service, a class, a conference or a church and there is sufficient relationship with the others attending to be a good spectator.

Actually, anything more than casual relationship can get in the way of being a good spectator. After all, when you go to a movie you don't go to get to know the people sitting next to you. That would keep you from watching the movie. You simply join others to view the movie.

For disciple-makers friendship not membership is primary. This is more than casual association through attendance. Friendship speaks of "constant association" with others in a common interest.[2]

Mark 3:13–15 says,

> *"Jesus went up on a mountainside and called to him those he wanted, and they came to him. He appointed twelve – designating them apostles – that they might be with him and that he might send them out to preach and to have authority to drive out demons."*

Here Jesus calls His disciples to preach, deliver from demons and heal the sick. But above all this He calls them to be with Him. This is not an invitation into a casual association. It is a call to be His friends.

Jesus, the one who ushers in the kingdom, has the right to call the twelve disciples to be with Him. But do you have the right to invite people to be with you in deep association for the sake of the kingdom?

Look at Acts 1:21. The disciples are going to select someone to take the vacant place of Judas. Notice the characteristic Peter is looking for in this person. Peter said, *"it is necessary to choose one of the men who has been with us."* They didn't just want someone who had been with Jesus. They were looking for a person who had been in deep association with *them* as a friend. The kingdom comes within the context of friendships with other disciples as well as with Jesus. Seek this level of association with others as much as the original disciples sought for it. Let's look at why friendship is the essential relationship for disciple-makers.

Truth through Friendship

Disciples must learn the truth of the kingdom. Kingdom knowledge doesn't come primarily through the study of information. Essentially it comes through being with those who live the truth of the kingdom.

When spectators want to learn they join other spectators in a class, seminar, school or service. They establish a casual association with a group of learners. Knowledge comes through the transfer of information from a teacher or a book to each class member. A student is a spectator who wants to learn.

A disciple goes much further. He or she seeks kingdom truth through friendship with Jesus and His disciples. They value being fully with others because kingdom truth travels best on the lines of relationship. In Acts 1:21 Peter was not looking for a scholar who had mastered Jesus' teachings. He wanted someone who had been with them as a friend and learned kingdom truth relationally. Later on Jesus' disciples were identified in Acts 4:13 as *"unschooled, ordinary men"* who knew what they knew because they had *"been with Jesus."*

Does this mean Bible schools, classes or seminars are wrong? No it doesn't. There is an important level of learning that comes by being a member of a class, school or church, but for this information to have maximum impact there must be deep association with others. Truth is transferred best through strong relationships.

Why is deep association the primary means of kingdom truth? Truth in the kingdom of God is not a curriculum but a life. Life-to-life transference provides the strongest environment for receiving this truth. It is not the only way to learn truth, but truth comes best through deep relationships.

Acts 19:20 says, *"the word of the Lord spread widely and grew in power."* How could the word of God spread and multiply in the New Testament Church? These people didn't have access to the printed word in their assemblies. Many of them couldn't read or write. They could not even pull together for large classes or schools. Wolfgang Simson explains, "The Greek word often translated 'preaching' in the New Testament is *dialogizomai*, which means to have a dialogue between people."[3] He goes on to share, "In technical terms, the eastern teaching style is kinetic: the topic of discussion literally moves around the table from person to person and everyone is involved."[4]

The word of God spread because truth was understood through relationships. It was not downloading information from a book or curriculum. Truth was taught, preached and dialogued into the people through deep association. It spread through life-to-life transference. In John 15:15 Jesus speaks of this way of learning. He says, *"I have called you friends, for everything I learned from my Father I have made known to you."* In deep association with the disciples He taught them what He had learned from deep association with the Father.

I spent three years as a member of a student body at seminary studying how to do ministry from books and curricula, but my most significant understanding of kingdom ministry didn't happen in a classroom. It took place in an old Dodge van. I was traveling the dusty back roads of Mexico with a Pentecostal lay missionary. In the deep association with "Brother Jim" on those mission trips I learned more about kingdom ministry than any class ever offered. It came through dialogue and practice in kingdom truth concerning the work of the Holy Spirit.

Kingdom truth is learned through life-to-life transference. Friendship offers the best connection for the transference of this truth.

Maturity through Friendship

Disciples of Jesus must also mature in the values of the kingdom. The way into maturity is with a group of friends committed to live for the kingdom together.

Proverbs 18:24 says,

> *"A man of many companions may come to ruin,*
> *but there is a friend who sticks closer than a brother."*

You can have many surface associations and still come to ruin. Casual companions do not affect your values. However, if you have close companions who will stick with you through the good times and bad they can affect your life. "Sticking" with a few others helps you mature in the values of the kingdom. This is the same word used in Genesis 2:24 for a man cleaving to his wife. Here is a deep relationship of loyalty and affection developed over long hours together.[5]

When Jesus invited two disciples to join Him in John 1:37–39, they went and hung out with Him the rest of the day. It was an invitation for them to start associating with Him for the sake of the kingdom. This friendship created a bond that was stronger than biological relationships. Later, in Mark 3:34, Jesus recognized these same disciples as being closer than family members. When friends stick like this through life's experiences, they have the ability to speak into your life.

This type of friend can draw out the best in you. When they know how you live and what desires you have, they can encourage you into your kingdom destiny. This "sticking closer than a brother" represents hours together that give friends unusual insight and wisdom to draw a fellow disciple into maturity.

C.S. Lewis explains that, in order to mature, you not only need one friend, you need several friends. He says, "In each of my friends there is something some other friend can fully bring out. By myself I am not large enough to call the whole man into activity: I want other lights than my own to show all his facets."[6] Maturity and wisdom grow out of deep associations.

Friends can effectively deal with your weaknesses. Proverbs 27:6 explains,

> *"Wounds from a friend can be trusted,*
> *but an enemy multiplies kisses."*

Friends have the right to say things that may hurt. They can point out your weaknesses so you can mature in kingdom values. This hurt is not done with evil intent. On the contrary, it is done with good intent to bring you to a new place of openness to God. Friends want you to deal with things you don't see, even if it hurts to see them.

Having friends who love you enough to tell you the truth, even if the truth hurts, is much better than living with people who kiss you with compliments. Your values will never be transformed if those close to you simply give you compliments in the midst of your weaknesses and sins. Friends tell you the hard things because they want to see you mature in the kingdom. Disciple-making offers the matrix of friendship for growth in kingdom values.

Vision through Friendship

Being with each other in deep association releases vision for the kingdom. If you want a friend you don't go and ask someone to be your friend. Friendship does not come through choosing a person. It comes through several persons choosing the same purpose and passion. Their gaze is not on the other persons but on the purpose they all seek. C.S. Lewis puts it well when he says, "Hence we picture lovers face to face but friends side by side, their eyes look ahead."[7] Looking ahead together they begin to have kingdom vision.

It begins when disciples look ahead to the Lord Jesus Christ in adoration. They worship together. Friends of the kingdom have no hesitation in expressing together their love for Jesus. Such worship brings the manifest presence of the Lord into their times with one another and increases their sensitivity to Him. Acts 13:2 shows five men in deep association worshiping the Lord and then vision came.

Deep association with Jesus and others produces vision for the expansion of the kingdom. Friends look ahead for God's purposes to be worked out in their lives. This was crucial with Jesus and His disciples. Toward the end of His ministry when He could draw bigger and bigger crowds, Jesus chose to spend more and more time with His disciples. He prayed with them, led them in retreats and in His last week spent all His time with them. Why? Vision doesn't manifest as you are with more and more people. It comes when you are with people more and more. Vision comes by deep association and looking ahead to God's purpose for your life.[8]

In John 15:27 Jesus says,

> *"And you also must testify, for you have been with me from the beginning."*

In other words, because they had been with Jesus in deep association, the vision was now in them to share with others. It came as they looked ahead together as friends.

When Paul left a church he didn't leave them with books, Bibles, tapes or manuscripts. So how were these people to get direction without those helps that are so important to us? Paul told them to draw together in deep association, worship the Lord and look ahead to Jesus. The Lord would speak and give them vision and strategy for their next step.

Some of the greatest points of vision in my life have come through being with other disciples in deep association. Early in my ministry I started meeting and praying with a fellow pastor. We didn't know where our little meeting would take us. Over the months God put in both of us a burning vision for missions. Eventually we left with our families and headed into a season of missionary work. The vision for such a move was born out of the deep association of kingdom friends.

Inter hominem esse is the Latin phrase for "being alive." It literally means "to be among men." "To be dead" is expressed in Latin by the phrase *inter hominem esse desinere*, which literally means "to cease to be among men."[9] In spectator Christianity it is possible to be in church and not be with friends. Without deep association you will be dead to the potential of kingdom breakthrough.

Jesus called the disciples to be with Him. This invitation was an invitation to life through deep association with Him and with one another. Out of those friendships the truth, values and vision of the kingdom exploded into the disciples' lives. This same life-to-life transference is still the best way to make disciples for the kingdom of God.

Notes

1. Wolfgang Simson, *Houses that Change the World* (Waynesboro: OM Publishing, 1999), p. 256.
2. Robert Coleman, *The Master Plan of Evangelism* (Grand Rapids: Fleming H. Revell, 1963), p. 43.
3. Simson, *Houses that Change the World*, p. 84.
4. Ibid., p. 85.
5. Ajith Fernando, *Reclaiming Friendship* (Leicester: InterVarsity Press, 1991), p. 15.
6. C.S. Lewis, *The Inspirational Writings of C.S. Lewis* (New York: Inspirational Press, 1960), p. 246.
7. Ibid., p. 249.
8. Coleman, *The Master Plan of Evangelism*, p. 44.
9. Mihaly Csikszentmihalhi, *Flow* (New York: Harper and Row, 1990), p. 165.

Chapter 4

Cause Each Other to Obey

"Make disciples ... teaching them to obey ..."
(Matthew 28:20)

"Each of you must put off falsehood and speak truthfully to his neighbor ..." (Ephesians 4:25)

"The gospel of Christ knows ... no holiness but social holiness." (John Wesley)[1]

Crises of Disobedience

Obedience to Jesus is the heart of what it means to be His disciple. Unfortunately there is an epidemic of disobedience in the Church. Today many believers are not choosing a kingdom lifestyle. Instead, they reflect the lifestyle of our culture. It is becoming more and more difficult to distinguish the life of the believer from the life of the unbeliever.

This epidemic of disobedience comes largely out of spectator Christianity. In spectator Christianity obedience is personal. As a spectator you alone are responsible for obeying Jesus. A sermon or an inspiring event can help you obey, but ultimately obedience is between you and Jesus. Quite frankly that is why spectator Christianity is not working.

In disciple-making Christianity, however, obedience is not solely dependent on you. Your obedience also depends on those with whom you have relationship. Consistent obedience comes through relationship with others.

Jesus introduced a new style of discipleship to transform people for kingdom breakthrough. He developed a strongly relational discipleship that empowered people to choose for the kingdom of God. Mortimer Arias said, "Jesus left behind two things: the message of the kingdom and a community of disciples."[2] These two things are bound together. Obedience to His message comes through a community of disciples causing each other to obey.

Can you obey Jesus without being in relationship to others? Yes and no. You can obey the elementary dimensions of the kingdom, but to obey fully means embracing relational Christianity. For this reason John Wesley said, "Solitary religion is not to be found there [the Gospel]. 'Holy solitaries' is a phrase no more consistent with the Gospel than holy adulterers. The Gospel of Christ knows no religion but social; no holiness, but social holiness."[3] In other words, there are levels of obedience you or the people you disciple will never choose unless you travel together. Obedience is not a private, isolated affair. It is born out of relationship in three different ways.

Moved to Obey

Disciples cause each other to obey through the empowerment of the Holy Spirit. In our own strength we can't consistently and passionately choose for God. But the Holy Spirit can empower our wills to choose for God even if it means choosing against our selfish desires. In Ezekiel 36:27 God promised the coming of the Holy Spirit to help us obey. He said,

> *"I will put my Spirit in you and move you to follow my decrees and be careful to keep my laws."*

He didn't say the Spirit will make us keep His laws. Instead, He will empower us to do so.

In much of spectator Christianity the only work of Holy

Spirit empowerment is a personal experience. The infilling of the Holy Spirit can come at a service or in some private seeking of the Lord, but it is a personal impartation of Holy Spirit power into your life. Through this personal experience the Spirit empowers you to obey.

When personal experience is the only impartation of power and you fall into disobedience after that personal experience, you then must seek another personal experience. To depend only on personal experiences for your obedience can cause great disappointment when those experiences are not creating lasting obedience.

There was a time in my life when I made disappointing trip after trip to the altar of the church trying to find the personal experience that would "knock the ball out of the park" and bring me to continuous obedience. Unfortunately, this spectator view of holiness created ongoing frustration.

In disciple-making Christianity obedience comes not just through a personal experience of the Spirit's power into your life. It comes also through a relational impartation of the Spirit. Through the Spirit's power everyone causes each other to obey. The personal event of being filled with the Holy Spirit gives a seismic change toward holy living. However, if you do not couple this with the ongoing aftershocks of relational sanctification, you will not enter the full dimension of kingdom obedience.

Bruce Milne explains,

> "The bulk of New Testament teaching on the Christian life, including the major sections on holiness, occur in letters addressed to corporate groups, to churches. All major exhortations to holy living are plural – 'we', 'you' (Romans 6:1–23; Galatians 5:13–6:10; Ephesians 4:17–6:18). Similarly all the New Testament promises of victory are corporate (1 Corinthians 15:57; 1 John 5:4; Revelation 15:2). In other words the Apostles envisage the Christian life and Christian sanctification in the context of a loving caring fellowship."[4]

We can best cause each other to obey in the setting of relationships.

A personal impartation of the Spirit's power is essential. But you must also have an ongoing relational impartation of God's power. This is not to take away from the importance of any personal experience of the Holy Spirit. It is simply to give yourself fully to what God is doing through that experience. As people gather together to pray for one another God releases more of His power through His body. This helps everyone to choose consistently for the kingdom. Paul reminds us in Ephesians 1:23 that the church, our relationship together in Christ, is *"his body, the fullness of him who fills everything in every way."* The sanctifying power of the Holy Spirit fills you through the event of faith and surrender, as well as through your relationship with other disciples.

Teach Them to Obey

As a disciple-maker you also cause each other to obey through teaching. How do you teach them to obey what Jesus said? In spectator Christianity people learn to obey through information. As believers learn everything Jesus said and taught, they expect to obey it. Often in spectator Christianity the Great Commission is quoted as "teach them everything *I* commanded." That is not what it says. That is the Great Omission. Jesus said, *"Teach them **to obey** everything I commanded."* Spectators spend much time learning what Jesus commanded rather than learning how to obey what He commanded.

This raises the questions: How do you teach people to obey? Will they become more obedient because they learn more of Jesus' commands? There is a level of learning obedience that comes from assimilating truth, but learning to obey is primarily relational. Yes, disciples need to learn what Jesus commanded. Obedience, however, does not come from education. It comes from training, which is relational learning.

Jesus' invitation to the disciples was not to join a seminar or learn the ten steps to be a disciple. His invitation was to follow

Him. He knew that, if these men could spend time with Him, He would eventually train them to obey what He wanted. They would learn to obey even the hard truths, such as dying to self. Jesus' method was kingdom training, not kingdom education. The way into obedience is not just sitting in front of a classroom lectern or a pulpit. If such education is not coupled with relationship to those who will cause you to obey, there will be very little obedience.

Teaching children how to obey happens through parents and family. A child learns to obey through a rich relational network. With the breakdown of the family in Western culture children are fatherless and parents are too busy for relationships. There is now an attempt to teach values in the school. Even though classroom values help, they are insufficient to cause children to obey. Without the relational network of the family it is hard to learn obedience.

In the same way the Church in the West has been fatherless and motherless. We have taught the values of the kingdom from pulpits but we haven't invested in one another relationally. Believers are not being trained into kingdom life. In disciple-making Christianity obedience to Jesus' commands comes from learning His commands and from training one another to obey. That is relational learning.

Accountable to Obey

We learn to obey through accountability. We all need an outside voice to keep us honest about our behavior. There is a simple reason for that. We have an incredible capacity to deceive ourselves. You can think you are living OK when in reality you are living in disobedience. This self-deception can come from strongholds of dysfunction. Live with these strongholds long enough and you are no longer aware of them. At other times, self-deception can come from a conscience that has been silenced through continuous disobedience.

Because of these blind spots we need an outside voice to keep us accountable. Otherwise we won't live out what Jesus commanded. Accountability is essential if believers are to become disciples. People obey through accountability.

ᐧJames recognized this problem in believers. In James 1:22–24 he says,

> *"Do not merely listen to the word, and so deceive yourselves. Do what it says. Anyone who listens to the word but does not do what it says is like a man who looks at his face in a mirror and, after looking at himself, goes away and immediately forgets what he looks like."*

You can see yourself in the mirror but, when you walk away, it is easy to forget what you saw.

Disciple-making Christianity has a way to make sure you don't forget what you saw in the word. It is relational accountability. The people around you hold you to the commands of Jesus by caring, praying and believing for you to obey. The word of God can be a powerful outside voice. But without the honest voice of some key people around you, you may not obey what the word has convicted you to do.

In early Methodism this accountability was the way people were taught to obey. John Wesley, describing the believers in his small groups, said, "They wanted to pour out their hearts without reserve, particularly with regard to the sin which did still easily beset them and the temptations which were most apt to prevail over them."[5] To join one of these groups a person had to answer some questions. "Do you desire that we should tell you whatsoever we think, whatsoever we fear, whatsoever we hear concerning you? Is it your desire and design to be on this and all other occasions entirely open, so as to speak everything that is in your heart without exception, without disguise and without reserve?"[6]

This kind of relational accountability kept the early Methodists in obedience so that they experienced more and more kingdom life. They were able to change a nation through their transformed lives. Their mission was to spread scriptural holiness across the land. Their method was to meet together and cause each other to obey.

The epidemic of disobedience in the Church today is rooted in our failure to teach people to obey. Even if we teach them everything that Jesus commanded, without a network of relationships people will not come into obedience. The epidemic of sins in the Church like pornography is not going to be overcome by simply teaching what the Bible says about unclean and impure lifestyles. It will only come when disciples join together to believe for the relational impartation of the Holy Spirit, learn how to obey, and hold one another accountable.

We only fool ourselves if we think we can get into kingdom life without discipleship. The verdict is in: spectator Christianity will not cause us to obey fully!

Notes
1. A fuller quote is given later in the chapter. See note 3.
2. Mortimer Arias, *Announcing the Reign of God* (Lima: Academic Renewal Press, 2001), p. 104.
3. Quoted in Peter Bunton, *Cell Groups and House Churches* (Ephrata: House to House Publications, 2001), p. 71.
4. C.J. Mahaney (ed.), *Why Small Groups?* (Gaithersberg: PDI Communication, 1996), pp. 5–6.
5. Quoted in Bunton, *Cell Groups and House Churches*, p. 64.
6. Mahaney (ed.), *Why Small Groups?*, p. 7.

Chapter 5

Do Jesus' Works Together

"Anyone who has faith in me will do what I have been doing."
(John 14:12)

"To each one the manifestation of the Spirit is given for the common good." (1 Corinthians 12:7)

"Everyone can play!" (John Wimber) [1]

Power through Community

Anointing is essential for kingdom disciples. As a disciple you are called to do what Jesus did. And Jesus did kingdom works. He did the works of the kingdom through the anointing of the Holy Spirit. You need this same power of the Holy Spirit to do these works. So how do disciples experience the power of the Holy Spirit?

Spectator Christians are convinced the power of the Holy Spirit comes primarily through anointed leaders. Spectators depend on gifted individuals who can do the works of Jesus. These leaders who have the power of the Holy Spirit bring anointing into the event that spectators attend. Spectators experience the Spirit's power through anointed leaders who teach, preach and minister.

Disciple-makers view anointing differently. Everyone gets to do the works of Jesus. In relational Christianity the primary anointing of the Holy Spirit doesn't come through a gifted individual. The Spirit's power comes through a gifted community.

Luke 9:1–2 reports,

"When Jesus had called the Twelve together, he gave them power and authority to drive out all demons and to cure diseases, and he sent them out to preach the kingdom of God and to heal the sick."

Here Jesus made a strategic move as a disciple-maker. He refused to be the unique individual with the Holy Spirit's power. Because Jesus had the Holy Spirit without measure He chose to impart the power of the Holy Spirit into His disciples. He then sent them out in pairs and encouraged them to do what He had been doing. Jesus gave the disciples a pre-Pentecost test drive of the Holy Spirit's power.

Jesus didn't want spectators who only observed Him doing anointed ministry. He wanted His disciples depending together on the Holy Spirit's power to do kingdom works. Jesus knew that a relational manifestation of anointing would be far stronger than any individual anointing, even His own. In spectator Christianity the primary expression of the Spirit's anointing is in a gifted individual. That is not so with disciple-making Christianity where the primary expression is in community. Relationships, in which everyone is depending on the Holy Spirit together, make the best environment for the Holy Spirit's power.

The Greater Anointing

If you do Jesus' works with other disciples, then your group will eventually manifest a more extensive anointing than a gifted individual. Jesus told His disciples in John 14:12 that whoever has faith in Him will do even greater works than He did. Did He mean His anointing through us is more powerful than through Him? Yes, but it is more powerful only in quantity not in quality. Think of it. As you read this paragraph, countless people around the world will be saved, healed, delivered and someone may even be raised from the dead because Jesus' anointing is in the community of believers and not in just one person. Today, through disciples worldwide, we see a more extensive work of Jesus' anointing. It is even more extensive than Jesus personally had in His earthly ministry.

Spectator Christians believe that one person ministers and everyone else receives. Disciple-makers say that everyone ministers and everyone receives. Although Jesus is the Christ, the Anointed One, He is not to be the only anointed person. Jesus made sure all His disciples believed for anointing. We are called Christians or "little anointed ones." Our combined little anointings create a more extensive work of Jesus than His one earthly anointing.

John Wimber, the primary leader in the early Vineyard movement, was a man under a powerful anointing. But he understood the priority of an anointed community over an anointed individual. He said, "We kind of had an 'everybody can play' attitude. I would say things like, 'Well, if you know the Lord at all, get up. Let's minister . . .' That sounded a little reckless but really all I was saying was, 'everybody can play'. Let's do it together. Everybody can worship, everybody can pray. Everybody can prophesy. Everybody can heal. Everybody can win the lost. Everybody can feed the poor and on and on."[2]

Wimber was simply echoing Paul's words in 1 Corinthians where he says gifts are given to God's people when they come together (12:11; 12:27; 14:26). Paul is saying that the greatest expression of gifts comes in the corporate setting, not in the individual. Therefore, do as Jesus did in Luke 9 and encourage all the disciples to play.

Is there a place for anointed leaders? Certainly there is. Some believers develop a strong gifting. They may have a powerful ministry in healing or the prophetic. These anointed leaders, however, are not called to gather a crowd of spectators and wow them with the flexing of their spiritual muscles. In Ephesians 4:11–12 Paul says that God does raise up anointed leaders like apostles, prophets, evangelists, pastors and teachers. Their ministry is not to entertain spectators with the greatness of their anointing. Instead, they are *"to prepare God's people for works of service, so that the body of Christ may be built up."*

Anointed leaders are not anointed in order to do the entire ministry. They are empowered to release others into Jesus' works. When that happens the anointing becomes exponential in its manifestation as it multiplies through relationships. Jesus told the Twelve to do what He did and then turned around and told the Seventy the same. He loved to see disciples depending on the Spirit together and doing what He did.

How easy is it for a community of disciples to break into a corporate anointing? It is so easy children can do it. Steve and Pam English are missionaries in Guatemala. They have a home where they take care of orphans and children with needs. Although Steve believes the Bible, he was raised in a church where they didn't pray for the sick. In their little orphanage they had three children with severe physical needs. Even though Steve hadn't seen healings in his own ministry, he knew it was in the Bible. For that reason Steve taught his kids what the Bible said and invited them to pray for their friends in need. The children began to pray. Eventually the three children that had physical needs were healed. Steve did not limit these little disciples to his experience. He released the community of children to do the works of Jesus. Anointing can come to any group of disciples, including children who believe and practice the works of Jesus.

The Best Place to Risk

A community of a few provides a safe place in which disciples can risk for the power of the Holy Spirit. Entering into the anointing can be very risky. It is unpredictable, uncertain and sometimes a little untidy. Like learning anything new, you will fail at doing the works of Jesus before you start to get it.

Even in Luke 9:40, after Jesus tells the disciples to do His works, there is a story of the disciples failing in an attempt to cast out a demon.

If you are going to risk for anointing, make sure you are in the best place in which to take the risk. In spectator Christianity the only place people can learn the gifts and ministry of the Holy Spirit is in an event with many other spectators. That is not a safe place in which to take risks because there is no opportunity for follow-up. Events are not the best place to release everyone to do the works of Jesus. That is why spectators often limit the works of Jesus to leaders.

You, as a disciple-maker, aim for a few. And that is the best setting in which to release people to do Jesus' works. Even though people still have to risk for the gifts of the Holy Spirit they are in an environment where there can be trust, encouragement and correction. Peter Horribon says that Jesus' strategy for training His disciples was this: "Listen to what I say and watch what I do, then have a try yourself. Then come back, tell me all about it and share your problems. Then listen to what I say and watch what I do."[3]

Jesus' whole paradigm of learning presupposes aiming for a few. You can't do this in a large gathering of spectators. You have to be committed to making disciples out of a few. As a matter of fact, after the disciples risked and failed at casting out a demon, we read in Mark 9:28–29 that Jesus and His disciples came together. Then Jesus answered their questions as to why the disciples missed the anointing.

Many spectators do not pursue the anointing because they don't have a safe place in which to risk for it. David Pytches explains, "The gifts are given us to use for others. They are developed in a climate of risk-taking and a willingness to fail. They are developed in an atmosphere where others may be observed exercising the gifts. The gifts do not come in an academic setting, they are not a cerebral exercise."[4] The relational Christianity of a disciple-maker provides the best place for risking into the anointing of the Holy Spirit.

Anointing for Revival

Disciple-making Christianity also provides the most intense corporate anointing that can be known: revival. Most of us think revivals are an event experience. But look behind the large gatherings and you will find a small group of people who have prayed, confessed or risked into a massive eruption of God's anointing. It was true in the early Church and has been true throughout church history.

A.T. Pierson explains, "From the day of Pentecost, there has been not one great spiritual awakening in any land which has not begun in a union of prayer, though only among two or three; no such outward, upward movement has continued after such prayer meetings have declined."[5]

Look at the Wesleyan revival in England. At first glance it appears to be an event revival where thousands gathered in open fields to hear John Wesley and others preach. Although these large gatherings were an important part of the Methodist revival, they were not the engine that drove the revival.

The energy came from the class meetings. These small groups of disciples produced the atmosphere for revival. Howard Snyder says, "The class meeting ... became the sustainer of Methodist renewal over many decades. The movement was in fact a whole series of sporadic and often geographically localized revivals which were interconnected and spread by the society and class network, rather than one continuous wave of revival which swept the country." Then Snyder concludes, "Without the class meeting, the scattered fires of renewal would have burned out long before the movement was able to make deep impact on the nation."[6]

There was also the great Moravian revival. It produced a prayer meeting lasting 100 years and launched one of the greatest missionary movements in church history. Where did the Moravian revival of 1727 start? Dr Kenneth Pfohl says that there were two distinct lines of preparation for this revival. "One was prayer," he said, "the other was individual work with individuals." He explains, "Men and women met for

prayer and praise at one another's home."[7] Disciple-making
Christianity ignited the Moravian revival.

Indeed, you need to be careful that anointed leaders do not
derail you from disciple-making Christianity and eventually
quench a more intense anointing for revival. In the early
1990s the Vineyard movement welcomed some highly
anointed prophets into their churches to minister through
conferences and events. Powerful transformations came out of
the ministry of these gifted prophets, but there was also a
subtle shift.

John Wimber explains this shift,

"During the period of the prophetic era and on into the
new renewal, our people quit starting small groups, they
quit prophesying, they quit healing the sick, they quit
casting out demons, because they were waiting for the big
bang, the big revival, the big thing . . . I thought, 'My God!
We've made an audience out of them. And they were an
army!' We in effect told them, 'You can't do anything. You
aren't talented enough. You're not gifted enough. You're
not holy enough. You're not prepared enough. Stand back
and let somebody who is, do it!' We did it, not so much by
precept but by example. In effect I said, 'Time out.' And it
went against everything I believed in, in terms of freeing
the church to minister."[8]

Don't let the anointed event or anointed leader distract you
away from the anointed people. Paul reminds us in Ephesians
1:23 that the Church, the anointed people, is the body of
Christ, the fullness of Him who fills everything in every way.
The most intense expression of anointing is in the relationships of God's people.

Signs and Wonders in Homes

I once heard a missionary share about an evangelistic cam-
paign that brought several hundred Russians to the Lord.

Everyone was invited to the next worship service of a local church in the Siberian town, but Communist city officials got wind of the conversions and told the church that they couldn't have any more public services. The missionary pleaded with the officials to let him meet with all the people corporately for ten minutes. The officials agreed. That Sunday the missionary had a number of people come to the front of the church. He then divided the crowd and assigned them to gather at the home of one of the people standing in front of them. After ten minutes everyone dispersed knowing there would be no more public meetings. They only met in the home where they were assigned. Nine months later the missionary got a call from one of the home leaders. The leader reported the home meetings were growing and multiplying rapidly because signs and wonders were breaking out in the groups.

What was an attempt to diffuse and control the church by the local Communist government actually forced it into the place of greatest anointing: disciple-making Christianity. As they depended together on the Spirit, God came in power. This is Jesus' method.

Notes

1. A fuller quote is given later in the chapter. See note 2.
2. Carol Wimber, *John Wimber: The Way It Was* (London: Hodder & Stoughton, 1999), p. 181.
3. Peter Horribon, *Healing Through Deliverance: The Practical Ministry* (London: Sovereign World, 1995), p. 32.
4. David Pytches, *Spiritual Gifts in the Local Church* (Minneapolis: Bethany House Publishers, 1985), p. 59.
5. Arthur Wallace, *In the Day of Thy Power* (Fort Washington: Christian Literature Crusade, 1956), p. 112.
6. Howard Snyder, *The Radical Wesley* (Downers Grove: InterVarsity Press, 1980), p. 57.
7. John Greenfield, *Power From On High* (Bethlehem: The Moravian Church in America, 1928).
8. Wimber, *John Wimber: The Way It Was*, pp. 180–181.

Chapter 6

Enable Everyone to Lead

"The one who rules [should be] *like the one who serves."*
(Luke 22:26)

"They have devoted themselves to the service of the saints."
(1 Corinthians 16:15)

"Every member is a potential leader."
(César Castellanos)[1]

Leaders Who Serve

Leadership for a disciple-maker is extremely important. It's important because every disciple is a potential leader. Such a thought among spectators is not only unimportant, it's impossible. Spectators define leadership so only a few can be leaders.

For a spectator the primary purpose of leadership is to govern. A few leaders govern many people. These select few manage the masses to become good followers. People are trained to follow, not lead. The idea of everyone becoming a leader is, therefore, impossible. In a gathering of many people, only a few leaders can govern.

Leadership for a disciple-maker is not to govern but to produce more disciple-makers. There is a massive difference between making disciples and making disciple-makers. If you are a leader who only makes disciples, then you govern people

to be faithful and obedient followers. The more followers you
manage, the greater your leadership skills. But if you are a
leader who raises up disciple-makers, not simply disciples,
then the few you lead will also become leaders. The more
leaders you multiply, the greater your leadership abilities.

Here are two different ways of leading. The few, who lead
many people, govern. Disciple-makers, who lead everyone to
become a disciple-maker, serve. Jesus told His disciples they
are not to lead like the world leads. He said,

> *"The kings of the Gentiles lord it over them; and those who*
> *exercise authority over them call themselves Benefactors. But*
> *you are not to be like that. Instead, the greatest among you*
> *should be like the youngest, and the one who rules like the one*
> *who serves."*   (Luke 22:25–26)

The greatest, or the leader, in the kingdom of God is a servant,
not a ruler. Serving is the way to make every disciple a leader.
How does a leader serve?

Lead as the Least

As a leader, serve by openness. Future disciple-makers must be
clean. They have to deal with personal problems that keep
them from effective leadership. The only way God can make
these potential disciple-makers clean is for them to be open
about their personal needs.

How do you get potential leaders to be vulnerable? Open
them up by being open with them. Serve them through
openness. Lead by openly sharing yourself. As your openness
allows God to heal you, these future leaders will want the
same for themselves. Henri Nouwen explains, "Laying down
your life means making your own faith and doubt, hope and
despair, joy and sadness, courage and fear available to others
as a way of getting in touch with the Lord of life."[2]

Leaders of spectators find it hard to be open with those they
lead. First, they are not in a setting to be fully open. A large

gathering is not the place for being vulnerable. Openness is best among the few. Leaders of many preach and teach to the many instead of opening up to them. Even if they do open up before a crowd the benefits of openness can't be realized. How can a large gathering speak into the leader's life?

Also, leaders of spectators are not in a position to be open. The power to govern is dependent on a positive image. That is one reason why organizations and leaders often seek a positive spin on information. Any openness of the leader that is negatively misunderstood by the many is hard to correct. If it hurts the leader's reputation, it will affect his or her power to govern. Leaders of many, therefore, are reluctant to share themselves openly with the many. They are concerned with creating positive perceptions.

Jesus taught that disciple-makers have a different concern than maintaining a good image. In Luke 9:48 He says, *"For he who is least among you all – he is the greatest."* Greatness or leadership in the kingdom is to be the least, the most vulnerable of the group. Whereas leaders of spectators govern by building a good image, you serve by making yourself of no reputation (Philippians 2:7). Honestly share who you are with your potential leaders. Such vulnerability welcomes the transforming power of the kingdom. When future disciple-makers see how your openness brings transformation, they too will open up for God's power to work in their lives.

Tommy Tyson stumbled into this kingdom truth with a small group reading about the coming of the Holy Spirit in Acts 2. Tommy desperately wanted to be filled with the Holy Spirit, but he feared that, if these men discovered how inadequate he was as a leader, they would lose respect for him. He would no longer have a ministry among them; consequently he had to guard his image.

Then the Lord spoke to him, "Do you want a ministry of your own making or do you want to be filled with the Spirit of God?" At that point Tommy was willing to become of no reputation in the eyes of those who accepted him as their leader. Becoming the least, he openly shared with them how empty he was and how much he needed what happened in Acts 2. While he was making a real mess of his confession, God began to fill him. Wave after wave of power transformed his inner life. This was the beginning of his true ministry![3]

Not only was Tommy filled with the Spirit but he served each of those potential leaders by being open with them in order to receive the transforming power of the kingdom. God meets needs when there is such vulnerability. Serve through openness.

Lead as the Youngest

Leaders serve by enabling future disciple-makers to do ministry. If disciples are going to make disciples they need to know how to minister to people. How do you get them into ministry? With spectators you don't. Ministry is the responsibility of one trained leader. That is the way spectators want it. They come to watch and will pay a leader to take care of their many needs. Only the paid leader ministers. Spectators receive ministry from the religious professional.

In disciple-making Christianity since everyone is a potential leader, everyone ministers. Jesus describes how to lead so future disciple-makers can minister. In Luke 22:26 He says, *"the greatest among you should be like the youngest."* In other words, the leader or the greatest among future disciple-makers leads by being the youngest.

What does He mean? Gayle D. Erwin explains the idea of "being the youngest" this way: "Being the younger is, by its nature, not a position of strength or authority. It does not speak dominance. It tends to be a position that wants and accepts whatever comes after others have had first choice."[4] You lead by preferring others to do ministry. Give them first crack at it.

This is good body life. Body life is designed to make leaders. Paul describes in 1 Corinthians 14:26 how our life together as a few should work. He says,

"When you come together, everyone has a hymn, or a word of instruction, a revelation, a tongue, or an interpretation. All of these must be done for the strengthening of the church."

Ministry among the few is participatory, spontaneous, inspired and interactive. This is the environment that strengthens the church because it develops more leaders.

Don't lead by monopolizing ministry. As the youngest, serve by making sure everyone has the opportunity to do ministry. Don't dominate and don't allow anyone else to dominate. Everyone ministers because everyone is a potential leader. Serve as the youngest by preferring others to minister.

Spectators believe you must have lots of experience, get trained and be called before you do ministry. Only the professional minister does it. How can the inexperienced, untrained and least gifted possibly do ministry?

In disciple-making Christianity, they not only can, they must! Become the youngest who gives it all away to those who know less than you. Jesus quickly released inexperienced, untrained people into ministry. Neil Cole explains, "Remember the Samaritan woman at the well (John 4:28–30; 39–42)? What about the Garasene demoniac set free and commissioned to stay behind (Mark 5:1–20)? Do you find it amazing that Matthew is a despised tax collector at one moment (Matt. 9:9), hosting an evangelistic outreach party the next (vv. 10–13), and then sent into the cities as an Apostle to preach the gospel just a few verses later (Matt. 10:2 ff.)?"[5] The few around you are the future disciple-makers who are released into ministry now. Train them up by giving them ministry.

Lead as the Servant

If you are going to make disciples into disciple-makers, don't just clean them up and train them up, but stir them up with a passion for the kingdom. If you are going to make leaders out of disciples, empower them with passion for the kingdom. In spectator Christianity the people support their leaders so

these leaders can do more ministry and govern more spectators. The people empower them with compensation, position,
title and encouragement.

Jesus warned about what this kind of support does to
leaders. He said,

> *"they love the place of honor at banquets and the most*
> *important seat in the synagogues; they love to be greeted in*
> *the marketplaces and to have men call them 'Rabbi.'"*
>
> (Matthew 23:6–7)

He goes on to explain to His future disciple-makers,

> *"But you are not to be called 'Rabbi,' for you have only one*
> *Master and you are all brothers. And do not call anyone on*
> *earth 'father,' for you have one Father, and he is in heaven.*
> *Nor are you to be called 'teacher,' for you have one Teacher, the*
> *Christ. The greatest among you will be your servant."*
>
> (Matthew 23:8–11)

In disciple-making Christianity it is not the people who
support the leader; it is the leader who supports the people
to become disciple-makers. Leaders serve in whatever capacity
is necessary in order to make disciples who make disciples. Be
a servant to the potential disciple-makers who are around you.
Turn the pyramid of authority upside down.

Serve by praying for them. This is the most significant way to
release them into their kingdom destiny. Joel Comiskey con-
ducted a survey of eight cell churches and interviewed 700 cell
leaders to find out why some cell leaders are able to evangelize
and make disciple-makers. What he found was astounding.
Being a successful disciple-maker has nothing to do with
gender, social status, age, marital status or education. It has
nothing to do with personality type or spiritual gift mix.[6]

The number one factor in being a successful disciple-maker
is prayer. Those leaders who spent ninety minutes in daily
prayer saw twice as much growth in their cells as those who

prayed thirty minutes a day. But, more importantly, he discovered the greatest factor in whether or not people become disciple-makers was related to how much the leader prayed for these potential disciple-makers. Comiskey said, "Cell leaders who pray daily for their members are far more likely to multiply cells than those who pray for them only once in a while."[7] There it is. Prayer changes disciples into disciple-makers.

Pour your life into those who will be future disciple-makers. Pray for each of them. Listen to their dreams and make plans with them. Minister and speak into their lives. Stir them up with the fire of the Holy Spirit and watch them change before your eyes until they too are making disciples.

The End of a Movement

In the early 1800s Methodism was the fastest-growing Christian movement in the United States. Fueled by the camp meeting revival there was rapid multiplication through the class meeting. It was a hot house for new leaders. A person could start out as a class member, become a class leader, then become a circuit rider. There was no limit. Even the first Methodist bishop in the United States, Francis Asbury, had come up through the disciple-making track.

By the late 1800s, however, at the general conference two subtle decisions were passed. These decisions exposed a significant plate shift in Methodism. It was changing from a disciple-making movement into a church of spectators. The general conference decided that attendance at class meetings should no longer be obligatory. To be a Methodist you just needed to attend the worship event. They shifted their base community from a group of a few to an event of many. The second decision was to start a theological seminary. The primary form of leadership was shifting from everyone a leader to only a few educated leaders who governed the many. The disciple-making discovery of John Wesley to aim for a few and enable the few to lead was quickly unraveling.

There will always be a gravitational pull away from disciple-making Christianity. Only as you enable everyone to lead can it continue to grow and multiply.

Notes

1. Quoted from one of the mission statements of César Castellanos' church in Bogotà.
2. Henri J.M. Nouwen, *In the Name of Jesus* (New York: The Crossroad Publishing Co., 1989), p. 43.
3. Tommy Tyson, "How I Was Baptized in the Spirit," *The Healing Line*, Christian Ministries, Inc., Jacksonville Fl. (May/June 2003).
4. Gayle D. Erwin, *The Jesus Style* (Cathedral City: Yashua Publishing, 1983), p. 89.
5. Joel Comiskey, *Home Cell Group Explosion* (Houston: Touch Publications, 1998), p. 27.
6. Ibid., p. 38.

Chapter 7

Find Seekers with Them

"The kingdom of heaven is like a net that was let down into the lake ... " (Matthew 13:47)

"Do not forget to entertain strangers ... " (Hebrews 13:2)

"Evangelism is the work of a community."

(Lawrence Khong)[1]

Evangelism Is Not a Four-letter Word

Evangelism is an important value for disciples of Jesus Christ. Mention the need for evangelism in a church, however, and 90 per cent of the believers will get a knot in their stomach. Most people freeze up when it comes to evangelism. Peter Wagner is convinced that only 10 per cent of believers have the gift of an evangelist. That's why the other 90 per cent feel uncomfortable. It is not their gift. As a disciple-maker, how do you bring people to do evangelism?

In spectator Christianity there is an attempt to make every believer an evangelist. Persons are encouraged to find a seeker, invite them to church or witness to them one on one. Evangelism in spectator Christianity is like teaching folks to fish with a fishing pole. The individual believer chooses the lure of an event, a method or a personality to hook seekers and reel them into faith.

When Jesus told the disciples He would make them fishers

of men, the image He had was not of an individual fishing
with a pole and lure. The disciples had just been fishing with
nets! Look at Matthew 4:18–19. It reports,

> *"They were casting a net into the lake, for they were fisherman.*
> *'Come, follow me,' Jesus said, 'and I will make you fishers of*
> *men.' "*

Jesus would mend the disciples into a relational net that
captures people for the kingdom. Disciples would find seekers
together. The relationships of the disciples became the net
that gathers seekers into the kingdom.

Christian Schwartz confirms this truth with a startling
discovery in his survey of churches around the world. A
church's size turns out to be the third strongest negative
factor in the growth of a church. Size is on a par with liberal
theology and traditionalism in its ability to work against
evangelism. But here is the astonishing finding. The growth
rate of churches slows down, not as a church decreases in size,
but as a church increases in size! The larger the church
the slower the growth rate. In fact, Schwartz concludes, "the
evangelistic effectiveness of mini-churches (51 in average
attendance) is statically 1,600% greater than that of mega-
churches (2,856 in average attendance)."[2]

It seems the rich, intimate relationship of community is the
best net to catch seekers. When the size of a gathering
increases the relational quality decreases. Evangelism
becomes an individual effort with less than impressive results.
The relational net is not only the best way to do evangelism,
for some it is the only way they will ever do it.

Greater Potential for the Catch

The relational net provides a greater possibility for catching
seekers than if you evangelize alone. In Luke 10:1–7 Jesus sent
out seventy disciples two by two. He told them to enter a
household. He was not just speaking of a literal house but of

the network of relationships the house represents. They were to go to the relational network. That is why He told them not to jump around from house to house. They were to go stay with folks and develop relationship.

Every believer already has a household of relationships where people connect through common ties or tasks. Within this network of relationships resides the best potential for bringing a seeker into the kingdom. We each have our personal household of eight to ten family members or personal friends, our extended household of 200 acquaintances and our potential household. This final category represents people you have a cultural right to relate to like neighbors and colleagues at work.[3]

In your relational network there are a few who don't know the Lord. Christian Schwartz suggests, "all Christians have about the same number of contacts with non-Christians in our relational network, which is about 8.5 contacts."[4] Out of these eight or nine unbelievers Jesus instructs us in Luke 10:5 to look for the person of peace. He is speaking about a true seeker. A seeker is a person who is open enough to consider the gospel. This greatly reduces the number of genuine seekers in our household of relationships. Out of those 8.5 contacts you have with unbelievers, maybe only a few contacts are ready to respond at some level.

However, if you survey the number of true seekers in the combined households of your discipleship group instead of those few seekers you know, the number increases ten times or more! Find them together and you have more potential seekers. Suddenly you have a lot of possibilities for evangelism.

At Yoido Full Gospel Church, South Korea, small groups of disciples are always finding seekers together and winning them to Jesus. How do they identify these seekers who will respond to their invitation? Karen Hurston says, "Find people with needs and problems and then lead them to the problem solver, Jesus Christ." One leader tells her group, "Look for problems. When you find someone with a problem, you are almost guaranteed that person will come to Jesus."[5] In the vast net of combined relationships in your group you increase the number of unbelievers with problems who are looking for the Problem Solver. Add one of these seekers into your relational net and they also bring their household of relationships.

Greater Success in the Catch

The relational net also gives greater success. When you evangelize together you suddenly have a greater mix of gifts to touch the lives of seekers. Think of it, if only 10 per cent of believers have the gift of an evangelist, that means not every group of disciples will have someone with this gift. Will they still be able to attract and win seekers to the kingdom?

Even if a group does not have a disciple with the gift of an evangelist, it still has a rich gift mix to meet the needs of different seekers. Some in the group will have the gift of hospitality to open up their home so that a seeker feels welcomed. Others will have the gift of mercy to encourage or minister to a seeker who carries a problem. There may be someone with the gift of faith to pray for the seeker's problem to be solved and to pray for his or her salvation. The gift of prophecy can be a means through which a seeker hears the voice of God for the first time. Paul says in 1 Corinthians 14:25 that a seeker will exclaim, *"God is really among you!"* when you use prophecy.

You may not be an evangelist but add your gifts to the gifts in others and there will an arsenal of gifts to bring seekers to Christ. Peter encourages the full expression of gifts in 1 Peter 4:10. He says,

> *"Each one should use whatever gift he has received to serve others, faithfully administering God's grace in its various forms."*

Be intentional in using all your gifts together and seekers will be caught. Doing evangelism together creates a fuller gift mix to bring seekers into the kingdom, even when you don't have someone with the gift of an evangelist.

There is also greater success because you not only present Jesus Christ in a message; you also present Him in a community. Spectators win seekers through a message, at an event or by personal witness. Yes, the gospel message is important but it is only one way to present Christ. If it is all we use, it will not always be enough. Many people also need to experience the dynamics of Christ's presence in community.

Spectator evangelism is good but it is only partial. It seeks to bring people to Christ only in the context of a message to believe. The early Church was successful in its evangelism because people were discovering the reality of their salvation both in the message of the gospel and the community of the kingdom. Salvation is personal but it is not private. We are not only to present a message to seekers, but we must present them with a community of the kingdom. One contemporary of the early Christians remarked that it was the "beauty of life that causes strangers to join the ranks." Finding seekers with a relational net presents a fuller expression of Christ in both message and community. This means greater success in the catch.

The Church Planting Movement is a rapidly multiplying work among indigenous people. Because people are being won to communities of ten to thirty disciples as well as to a message of truth, this movement is exploding across the earth. This is evangelism the way it was intended! One missionary reported from Western Europe, "In 1998 my wife and I started 15 new church cell groups. As we left for a 6 month stateside assignment last July, we wondered what we would find when we returned. It is wild! We can verify at least 30 churches now, but I believe that it could be two or even three times that many." Also in a four-year period (1993–1997) more than 20,000 people came to faith in Christ resulting in more than 500 new church plants in one area of China.[6] Find seekers together and you present the full gospel. They discover Christ in the message and in the community of the kingdom.

Greater Variety in the Catch

Find seekers together and your relational net will catch a variety of people: unbelievers, believers and disciples. Too often spectator Christianity evangelism reels in only one kind of catch, an unbeliever. The two most popular forms of evangelism among spectators are personal evangelism and event evangelism. In personal evangelism an individual witnesses to a seeker one on one. In event evangelism seekers who attend the event are invited to come to the Lord.

On the one hand, if the unbelievers do not respond to the invitation through a conversation or an event there is no way to hold them for further evangelism. On the other hand, if seekers become believers there is no way to hold them easily to be discipled. Either way there is no natural next step in the spectator model of evangelism. For that reason discipleship often becomes an option that is never chosen after a person is won to the Lord. However, the Great Commission mandates us to make disciples not just win the lost. If we win people without making them disciples it weakens the work of God's grace in their life.

So what is the best way to catch people with a variety of spiritual needs and to meet those needs? Jesus said in Matthew 13:47,

> *"The kingdom of heaven is like a net that was let down into the lake and caught all kinds of fish."*

Net fishing catches a greater variety of people than fishing with a pole. And it not only catches a greater variety, it holds them. In net evangelism a person belongs before she believes. A relational net can hold a person as he is deciding to come to Christ or is surrendering to become a disciple of Christ. By finding seekers together you hold them to be softened, won and eventually discipled.

Alpha is a ten-week course for evangelism designed around small groups. The Alpha course has discovered the power of evangelizing in groups instead of with individuals. Nicky Gumbal tells the story of a man who had not come to faith in Jesus but had been attending his small group for several weeks. When he went on a retreat with the group he was turned off by the teaching on the Holy Spirit. He left and said he would never return. The next week he showed up at his group again. When asked why he came back he responded, "I miss you guys." Several weeks later he came to faith in Christ. The net of relationship held him. He belonged before he believed but because he belonged, he eventually believed, became a disciple and then a disciple-maker.

Use a relational net and you will hold a variety of people with a variety of needs in order to meet those needs. Look at Peter. He had no powerful conversion experience like Paul on the Damascus Road. Instead it was a series of changes. Because he was held in a relational net with Jesus and the other disciples his varied needs were met. When he responded to the invitation of his brother Andrew to join the others with Jesus, he began to belong (John 1:40–42). Again he saw how sinful he was in the boat with Jesus and the other disciples. Here was his conversion (Luke 5:1–11). He was transformed another time when he was on a retreat with Jesus and the disciples. He confessed Jesus as Christ, the Son of the living God (John 21:15–19). After he failed miserably as a disciple he was brought back into relationship with Jesus and the others (John 21:15–25). There was his change at Pentecost when he was filled with the Holy Spirit in the upper room with other disciples (Acts 2:4). Over and over again, as he was held in the relational net with Jesus and the disciples, Peter's needs were met!

Find seekers together and over time you will bring all kinds of folks into your relational net. Once in the net it will hold them to soften, win and disciple them.

Notes

1. *The Apostolic Cell Church* (Singapore: Touch Ministries International Pte Ltd, 200), pp. 141–142.

2. Christian Schwartz, *Natural Church Development* (Emmelsbull: C & P Publishing, 1996), pp. 47–48.

3. David Finnell, *Life In His Body* (Houston: Touch Publications Inc., 1995), pp. 76–82.

4. Schwartz, *Natural Church Development*, p. 34.

5. Karen Hurston, *Growing the World's Largest Church* (Springfield: Gospel House Publishing, 1995), p. 104.

6. David Garrison, *Church Planting Movements* (Richmond: International Mission Board, 1999), p. 4.

Chapter 8

Guide Them to Multiply

"It came up, grew and produced a crop, multiplying ... "
(Mark 4:8)

"I planted the seed, Apollos watered it, but God made it grow."
(1 Corinthians 3:6)

"Addition can never keep pace with multiplication."
(Walter Henrichsen) [1]

Add or Multiply?

Growth comes from life. When divine life flows, growth takes place. There are, however, different views of growth. Spectators see growth only as addition. The event increases by more and more people attending. Bigger is better because it means people are being added and the addition of more spectators means church life is successful. Mega-churches are the most successful because they have added and maintained more people than other churches.

Disciple-makers view growth differently. It is not increase by addition, rather it is multiplication by reproduction. The key is not adding people but making disciples who produce more disciple-makers. Christian Schwartz argues that this is growth the way God intends. It is natural. He explains, "A tree does not keep getting bigger; it brings forth new trees, which in turn produces more trees." He goes on, "Just as the true

fruit of an apple tree is not an apple but another tree, the fruit
of a small group is not a new Christian but another group, the
fruit of a church is not a new group, but a new church . . . "[2]
And the fruit of a disciple-maker is not a bigger group of
disciples but new disciple-makers.

Growth by multiplication instead of addition has explosive
potential. The Church Planting Movement calls it "multiplicative growth" and defines it as "extraordinary growth
characterized by each part multiplying itself. Thus, two
may become four, and four may become eight to ten, etc.,
in multiplicative growth. This contrasts with incremental
growth."[3] Jesus refers to multiplicative growth in the parable
of the soils. He illustrates that when the environment is right
for reproduction, then the seeds will multiply. Jesus said,

> *"Still other seed fell on good soil. It came up, grew and
> produced a crop, multiplying thirty, sixty, or even a hundred
> times."*   (Mark 4:8)

For disciple-makers creating this environment for reproduction is more important than simply increasing the size of a
group. If multiplication is to take place through reproduction,
the environment must be right. Jesus promised in Mark 4:24
after the parable of the sower that *"with the measure you use, it
will be measured to you – and even more."* How do you make
disciples with what God has given you so that *"even more"*
disciple-makers are produced?

God Is the God of Multiplication

God's power is essential for reproduction. It is possible to
increase a crowd by simply using human methods. Multiplicative growth, however, must have God's power. Caesar
Fajarta, who has seen seventy groups of disciples multiply into
20,000 within ten years, declares, "God is the God of multiplication." In the church humans may be able to add but only
God can multiply.

In Mark 4:26–29 Jesus tells about a seed planted in the soil and, while the sower sleeps, *"the seed sprouts and grows, though he does not know how. All by itself the soil produces corn ... "* (vv. 27–28). Here Jesus is speaking of the power of life in the natural world. The power of life mysteriously causes reproduction. Likewise, it is the power of divine life in the kingdom that causes multiplication by reproduction.

How can you prepare the environment for God's power to be released in a group of disciples? Prayer is one way. As you pray God's power is imparted into those you disciple so they too produce disciple-makers. Multiplicative growth unlike incremental growth cannot happen without prayer saturating your multiplying efforts.

In 1993 there were only six Baptist churches in Cambodia. Over the next six years they multiplied to 200 churches representing 10,000 new believers. What was one of the important factors in that explosive growth? One person explains, "Over the past six years there has been more mobilized prayer for the people of Cambodia than any other time in their history." Another writer shares, "Prayer also characterizes the lives of the new church members, filling them with a strong sense of God's direct involvement in their daily affairs. Signs and wonders, such as exorcisms, healings and other acts of spiritual warfare, continue to be common place among the Cambodian believers."[4] Reproduction comes not by finding the right method of multiplying. It only comes as everyone prays for God's power to reproduce in the acts of multiplying.

Prayer is not the only factor that releases the power of God to reproduce. The word of God is also important. In Mark 4:8 the seed was able to multiply thirty, sixty or even one hundred times. Jesus identifies the seed in the parable as the word of God. As the word of God is introduced into believers' lives it releases the power of God for transformation and multiplication. In Acts 12:24, speaking of disciples multiplying, Luke says, *"the word of God continued to increase and spread."* It's really not about disciples multiplying. It is about the word of God multiplying through disciples who read, live and impart God's word.

There is a catalytic mixture of prayer and God's word that releases the power of God for multiplicative growth. Since God is the God of multiplication, pray for God's power and saturate yourself in the word of God. Then lead any future disciple-makers around you into these powerful realities.

Die to Multiply

Death to self is essential to reproduction. Only as you die to security, comfort and control will there be multiplication. Spectators like growth by addition because it brings great satisfaction. It gives an immediate sense of success. Multiplication is different. It demands a willingness to sacrifice the good and immediate in order to risk for the better and delayed. Multiplication is slow in the beginning with few signs of success. Jesus puts it this way in John 12:24,

> *"I tell you the truth, unless a grain of wheat falls to the ground and dies, it remains only a single seed. But if it dies, it produces many seeds."*

Sacrifice is dying to things you enjoy in order to reproduce more for the kingdom. Multiplicative growth comes out of this kind of sacrifice. Jeffrey Arnold, describing sacrifice that produces growth, says, "The history of the church demonstrates that risk and crisis usually accompany growth. Growth breaks into our settled patterns of communication. Growth interrupts the security of deep conversation and stable relationship. Growth requires deep levels of other-centered care."[5]

Sacrifice must be part of your identity as a disciple-maker from the beginning. Otherwise, when the time comes to multiply, you will not die to security, comforts and relationship to reproduce more disciple-makers. It is interesting that in Mark 3:14, when Jesus called the Twelve to be His disciples, in the very beginning He designated them as apostles. From the start they knew they were coming together to be sent out and to reproduce in others what Jesus put in them. They were not called to add to the few for the purpose of enjoying the success of an ever-increasing number of disciples. No! They were instead called to multiply. Multiplication would eventually mean death to their comforts, securities and relationships for the sake of the expanding kingdom.

There is another side of this truth. You either die to multiply or you refuse to multiply and eventually die. Increase by addition doesn't go on indefinitely, multiplication by reproduction can. Christian Schwartz, in his study of churches around the world, reveals there is no greater influence on the growth and quality of church life than to have groups that are willing to die to comforts in order to multiply. On the other hand, there is no greater factor for illness in a church than an organization that chooses comfort by blocking any multiplication in the church. He concludes, "What is the Great Commission if not a call for ongoing multiplication?"[6]

Dying to your comfort, security and control in order to multiply is a sacrifice. But it isn't the greatest loss. The greatest loss is not to sacrifice. If you don't sacrifice to enter into the promise land of multiplication, then you will wander in the desert of extinction. Multiply or die!

Simplify to Multiply

Simplicity is essential for multiplication. If you want to multiply through reproduction, don't complicate the process. When you require too much time, experience and knowledge before a disciple-maker can multiply, it steals simplicity. Reproduction in nature is very simple. No extensive education or experience is required to reproduce. Reproduction in the kingdom of God is also simple and spontaneous. The biggest reason it doesn't happen is that we make the process too complex.

One man in India who had recently come to the Lord planted forty-two churches in one year.[7] It wasn't because of the time he waited, or the experiences he accumulated. Neither was it the amount of knowledge he mastered. Rather, the man was given a simple process to produce new disciple-makers. Because he was in relationship with a supervising disciple-maker he could produce new disciple-makers even as he learned. Without this relationship to a supervisor, spectators must require time, a lot of experience and great knowledge before someone is trusted even to manage a group of disciples.

Simplicity affects reproduction because simplicity leads to rapid reproduction. Rapid reproduction means stronger multiplication. The Church Planting Movement found that rapid reproduction is essential. They explain, "When the rate slows down, the Church Planting Movement falters. Rapid reproduction communicates the urgency and importance of coming to faith in Christ. Where rapid reproduction is taking place you can be sure that the churches are unencumbered by nonessential elements . . . "[8] In other words simplicity helps rapid reproduction.

Unfortunately, if reproduction is not rapid it might not happen at all. Faith Community Church in Singapore has learned that, if cell groups of disciples do not quickly produce disciple-makers in order to multiply the group, it will never multiply. They explain, "Generally, the life span of any cell should be between six to nine months. We have discovered that any cell which does not multiply after about 12 months will usually stagnate, lose its life or dynamism and eventually die."[9]

Simplicity not only brings rapid reproduction, it causes extensive reproduction. Not every disciple will become a disciple-maker but if disciple-making is made simple enough many more disciples will become disciple-makers. And more disciple-makers producing disciple-makers means greater multiplication. Neil Cole reports, "that if a single shaft of wheat is left unmarred and blighted and allowed to freely produce and grow, within only eight years it will have multiplied into a crop large enough to feed the entire world population – for an entire year!"[10]

Obviously no shaft of wheat is going to multiply perfectly. Neither will any disciple-maker multiply perfectly. But if reproduction is simple, then more disciple-makers are produced than if reproduction is complicated. The more seeds produced, the greater the multiplication. Extensive multiplication happens when reproduction is made simple.

Popcorn Multiplication

In Guayaquil, Equador the International Mission Board of the Southern Baptist Church simplified church planting and released the people to be disciple-makers by gathering disciples and evangelizing people in their homes. In the movement La Iglesia En Tu Casa people are trained as they plant and evangelize. In the training course each person must start a church within the first four weeks! Manuel Sosa says, "It is a popcorn effect. We hear each week of churches that have been started that we didn't know anything about. We have no idea where they are popping up."

Chris Turner reports, "If simplicity is the framework upon which 'La Iglesia En Tu Casa' is hung, prayer is the foundation." He goes on to say that the disciple-makers are taught "that prayer and the Bible are their two greatest resources." Simplicity, prayer and sacrifice create the environment for multiplication.[11]

Notes

1. Quoted in *Cultivating a Life for God* by Neil Cole (St Charles: ChurchSmart Resources, 1999), p. 22.
2. Christian Schwartz, *Natural Church Development* (Emmelsbull: C & P Publishing, 1996), p. 68.
3. David Garrison, *Church Planting Movement* (Richmond: International Mission Board of the Southern Baptist Convention), p. 60.
4. Ibid., pp. 28, 29.
5. Jeffrey Arnold, *Small Group Outreach* (Downers Grove: InterVarsity Press, 1998), p. 43.
6. Schwartz, *Natural Church Development*, p. 69.
7. Garrison, *Church Planting Movement*, p. 56.

8. Ibid., p. 36.
9. Joel Comiskey, *Home Cell Group Explosion* (Houston: Touch Publications, 1998), p. 102.
10. Neil Cole, *Cultivating a Life for God* (St Charles: Church Smart Resources, 1999), p. 122.
11. Chris Turner, "La Iglesia En Tu Casa," *House to House*, Special Issue, copyright 2002.

Chapter 9

Help Them Succeed

"He appointed twelve – designating them apostles . . . "
(Mark 3:14)

"God has put us apostles on display at the end of the procession . . . "
(1 Corinthians 4:9)

"True Apostles are those who hide themselves rather than those who hustle themselves." (Frank Viola)[1]

Position or Posture?

Supervision is the right given a person to make sure another person succeeds. Once you have made disciple-makers and they have multiplied out with their own disciples, your relationships change. Now you help them succeed as new leaders. What does that supervision look like?

The main expression of supervision among spectators comes from position. Because some are given the position to superintend they have the right to direct, inspect and even control for the purpose of making sure others are successful.

As a disciple-maker your right to supervise does not come from a position you hold, but from a posture you take. It only comes when you communicate divine life to others. Supervision is not a job description. It is a lifestyle of faith and service.

You have the right to help other disciple-makers succeed,

but it only comes as you minister into them the truth and life of Christ. You have no inherent organizational right to direct or control disciple-makers you have raised up. Your right to supervise comes as you freely invest in them what Christ is freely giving to you.

In Mark 3:14 Jesus selects His disciples, *"designating them apostles."* One of the aspects of apostolic ministry is to help people and groups succeed for the sake of the kingdom. The first disciples were not just called to manifest the kingdom in their own group of a few and then they were done. They would be sent out to help other disciple-makers see kingdom breakthrough, but they were to do it in the apostolic style of the kingdom.

Although you may not be an apostle, as a disciple who has made disciple-makers you are called to apostolic supervision. Help them succeed but only out of an apostolic posture.

With Them, Not Over Them

How does apostolic supervision help people to succeed? In spectator Christianity supervisors rule over those they supervise. Because certain people have authority over other people they can command, demand or instruct those under them to do what needs to be done in order to see success. All the people need to do is listen to the supervisor's requirements and obey.

As an apostolic supervisor you are not over disciple-makers. You are with them. Paul declares in 2 Corinthians 1:24,

> *"Not that we lord it over your faith, but we work with you for your joy, because it is by faith you stand firm."*

This concept was so important to Paul that he was constantly inventing new words prefixed by the preposition "with" to demonstrate his identification with those he supervised.[2]

Floyd McClung, speaking of these apostolic supervisors who minister alongside those they help, said, "Their actions proceed from an attitude of equality, not authority because they are more concerned with serving than ruling."[3] Why should you take a position of "with" instead of "over?" Isn't success guaranteed if you just demand that people do what you know they need to do in order to succeed? Why is it that Paul is more interested in persuading those he cares for with words and deeds than demanding they do what he requires?[4]

Disciple-makers must learn to hear and know the voice of God if they are going to succeed. When all they hear is a supervisor's overriding, authoritative voice that demands obedience to a list of requirements, they will not hear the voice of God. However, if you walk beside them persuading them, they have the opportunity to hear the Lord and see if He is speaking through your words. Disciple-makers' continued success does not depend on obeying a supervisor but on obeying the voice of God. Above all, respect how God works in those you help.

In short, spectator supervisors believe they are the ones who guide the people they want to succeed. Apostolic supervisors know God is the one who guides and they do all they can to help others succeed in hearing God's voice.

Supervise for the Kingdom's Expansion

As an apostolic supervisor you should not only be concerned with how you supervise but why you supervise. The main reason spectators supervise is to build their ministry. Because spectators are concerned with growing the event and adding more people, they help others to succeed so it expands their personal ministry. The only way they see the extension of the kingdom is in the framework of their ministry.

Disciple-makers don't seek primarily to build their ministry. They want the expansion of the kingdom more than they want the increase of their ministry. That means their core concern is not getting some personal benefit out of supervising others. Rather, apostolic supervisors desire above any personal benefit the expansion of the kingdom through the lives of those they supervise. Frank Viola declares, "Real apostles do not build denominations, programs, missions, buildings or organizations; they exclusively build the *ekklesia* of Jesus Christ."[5]

The kingdom of God is greater than the sphere of your ministerial influence. Be more committed to God's ever-expanding kingdom than your own personal ministry. Gladly invest in others to succeed even if it brings no enhancement to your own ministry. Seeking to control all the disciple-makers you supervise so that they only add to your personal ministry stifles the spontaneous expansion of the kingdom of God.

Rolland Allen, declaring we should welcome a work greater than that which we can control, said,

> "By spontaneous expansion I mean something which we cannot control. And if we cannot control it, we ought, as I think, to rejoice that we cannot control it. For if we cannot control it, it is because it is too great, not because it is too small for us. The great things of God are beyond our control. Therein lives a vast hope. Spontaneous expansion could fill the continents with the knowledge of Christ: our control cannot reach as far as that."[6]

A ministry devoted to the ever-expanding kingdom of God at the expense of personal benefit is apostolic. In the interior of India, the predominately Baptist church growth movement among the Bholdari people grew so fast that the Southern Baptist Church couldn't assimilate into their denomination all the churches that were rapidly multiplying. In 1993 churches multiplied from twenty-eight to thirty-six. But by 1998 churches began multiplying themselves so that over 2,000 churches existed. The missionary from the International Mission Board of the Southern Baptist Church who was supervising this explosive growth chose not to spend time reining the churches into his denomination. Instead, he helped to form multiple alliances committed to the Bible as their undisputed authority. This kept the emphasis on church multiplication and not on building a denomination. He refused to control the growth to benefit only his denomination.[7]

When the goal is the spontaneous expansion of the kingdom you can transfer the work totally into the lives of disciple-makers. If the goal, however, is to benefit your ministry it will never go beyond the limits of what you can control.

Any Time Instead of All the Time

When does apostolic supervision happen? For spectators, supervision is either all the time or none of the time. The one extreme is to have a strong presence over those being supervised using rules and regulations to conform them to a mold. The other extreme is to totally abandon the people because they no longer serve the supervisor's ministry nor conform to the supervisor's mold.

In apostolic supervision it is neither all the time nor none of the time. It is any time. Help them succeed any time they need your encouragement. You are there for them but not there over them all the time. Too much supervision and they will never learn to depend on the Lord. Rolland Allen explains this aspect of apostolic supervision when he says, "To leave new born churches to learn by experience is apostolic, to abandon them is not apostolic: to watch over them is apostolic, to be always nursing them is not apostolic: to guide their education is apostolic, to provide it for them is not apostolic."[8]

The supervision of a spectator is like teaching a child to read. The supervisor must stay with him and direct him until he gets it. Apostolic supervision is more like a parent helping a child to walk. The parent watches and helps but most of all gives her freedom to walk. The child will walk if she is allowed to walk because walking is in the child.[9]

Multiplication is in the disciple-maker. The multiplication of disciples is a work of the Holy Spirit. As a supervisor don't smother disciple-makers with your control. The Holy Spirit will teach them. Simply give them room to go for it and be there if they need help.

As parents trust nature in children to cause them to walk, trust the Holy Spirit in believers to cause them to multiply. Be there when needed but not all the time. As an apostolic supervisor be there any time you can be a help. The key is care not dominance. Joel Comiskey, exploring the amount of meetings a supervisor should have with disciple-makers, explains that meetings are not what you measure. He says, "The number of meetings is not the issue. The key question is whether or not your cell leaders are receiving sufficient pastoral care and ministry. Determine what will accomplish the goal of caring for the cell leaders and put that system into place. Don't get stuck on the number of meetings."[10]

Spectator supervisors swing between supervising all the time or none of the time. Neither is apostolic. Choose to supervise any time you can help disciple-makers succeed in their ministry. Robert Banks discovered this same apostolic insight in Paul for his disciple-makers. He explains, "from the very beginning Paul recognizes their self-sufficiency in the Spirit, even though in some areas they may still need his assistance."[11] That is the heart of apostolic supervision.

Low-profile Footman

Paul himself explains this position of apostolic supervision well in 1 Corinthians 4:9. He says, *"For it seems to me that God has put us apostles on display at the end of the procession . . . "* If that is where God has put us, that is where we ought to stay!

In 1998 the International Mission Board saw the phenomenal multiplication of nearly 200 Cambodian Baptist churches in six years. The IMB missionary team that was in the country refused to take an assertive, authoritarian role. One of the team members encouraged these apostolic supervisors to "earnestly seek to become the low-profile footman" and "avoid the temptation of being a high profile front-man."[12] Help them succeed for the sake of the kingdom and learn to minister at the end of the procession.

Notes

1. Frank Viola, *Who Is Your Covering?* (Brandon: Present Testimony Ministry, 1999), p. 92.
2. Robert Banks, *Paul's Idea of Community* (Peabody: Hendrickson Publishers Inc., 1998), p. 178.
3. Larry Kreider, *The Cry for Spiritual Fathers and Mothers* (Ephrata: House to House Publications, 2000), p. 76.
4. Banks, *Paul's Idea of Community*, p. 176.
5. Viola, *Who Is Your Covering?*
6. Roland Allen, *The Spontaneous Expansion of the Church* (Eugene: Wipf and Stock Publishers, 1997), p. 13.
7. David Garrison, *Church Planting Movements* (Richmond: International Mission Board, 1999), pp. 23–25.
8. Allen, *The Spontaneous Expansion of the Church*, pp. 150–151.
9. Ibid., p. 151.
10. Joel Comiskey, *Groups of 12* (Houston: Touch Ministries, 1999), p. 96.
11. Banks, *Paul's Idea of Community*, p. 175.
12. Garrison, *Church Planting Movements*, p. 130.

Chapter 10

Go for the Kingdom

"Any of you who does not give up everything he has cannot be my disciple."   (Luke 14:33)

"Do not conform any longer to the pattern of this world ..."   (Romans 12:2)

"Every new step in the kingdom costs us everything we have gained to date ..."   (John Wimber)[1]

Final Orders

There is a cost in being a disciple-maker. In Matthew 28:19–20 Jesus' final marching order is clear. To all of us who call ourselves disciples of His kingdom, He says,

> *"Go and make disciples of all nations, baptising them in the name of the Father and of the Son and of the Holy Spirit, and teaching them to obey everything I have commanded you."*

In other words, make disciples who make disciples.

The fact is that many believers are not obeying Jesus' command to produce disciple-makers because the price is too high. The Western Church has settled for spectator Christianity. Jesus' words have been mutated to declare, "Attend and be a good spectator, get baptized and listen to everything I have commanded." Spectator Christianity has produced a lethargic

89

church compared to the vibrant multiplying church in other parts of the world and throughout church history.

Yet, even as we are waking up to the weak way we do church, many spectators still refuse to become disciple-makers. Maybe you are having a difficult time personally choosing for relational Christianity. You understand that spectator Christianity is not working. So what keeps you from choosing to be a disciple-maker? There are three basic reasons why spectators remain where they are, even when they recognize it is not the best place or the place of obedience. Are these reasons keeping you from paying the price to be a disciple-maker?

Pleading Ignorance

Some are not disciple-makers because they don't know how. The Gospels are a record of what Jesus said and also what He did. Jesus showed us the lifestyle of a disciple-maker. We also get those patterns within Acts and the first generation of disciples. Still, with all this truth, many believers don't know how to make disciple-makers. Why?

They don't know how because the Western Church has not accepted disciple-making Christianity. That means you may have never been discipled to be a disciple-maker. You have sat in church services, Sunday school, seminars and conferences but you have never had a small group of disciples to invest in you and make you a disciple-maker. It isn't something that has been modeled for you.

Does your ignorance of how it happens give you a legitimate excuse for not becoming a disciple-maker? Is doing something you've never experienced too great a price to pay?

Brother Yun of China shares about his mother's disadvantages in becoming a disciple-maker. She not only didn't have someone to disciple her, she couldn't even read or write. Brother Yun, explaining how she became a disciple-maker of some of the strongest leaders of house churches in China, says,

"She led a small church in our house. Although my mum couldn't remember much of God's word, she always exhorted us to focus on Jesus. As we cried out to him, Jesus helped us in his great mercy. As I look back on those days I am surprised how God used my mother despite her illiteracy and ignorance. The direction of her heart was totally surrendered to Jesus. Some of today's great house church leaders in China first met the Lord through my mother's ministry."[2]

You do not have to be discipled to be a good disciple-maker. You have a greater advantage than Brother Yun's mother. Maybe you weren't discipled but you can read and write. Pay the price. Find a group of people who want to experience relational Christianity. Cry out to Jesus and He will give you the direction. Even if you don't know how, you can still go for the kingdom with others because Jesus is the one who makes you a disciple-maker.

Too High a Price

Here is another reason why spectators do not fulfill the final command of Jesus. It is not just that believers don't know how to make disciple-makers, it's that they feel it is too uncomfortable. Their excuse is not ignorance but discomfort.

Many believers ignore Jesus' call because it just doesn't feel good. Let's be frank, Jesus' command to make disciple-makers is a call to a value system that runs cross-grain with Western culture. So, many spectators choose to stay where they are. Disciple-making is seen as an option for people in other places or, at best, something we can only fulfill through missionaries.

Do you value radical individualism more than the call of Jesus to make disciples? Do you want your comforts more than relational Christianity? Jesus beckons you to be committed to a group of people that evangelize and mature together in the things of the kingdom. Because His call can cost us some of our selfish cultural values, many spectators refuse to choose relational Christianity. Luke 9:23–24 reveals the price of being a disciple-maker. Jesus says without any spin,

> *"If anyone would come after me, he must deny himself and take up his cross daily and follow me. For whoever wants to save his life will lose it, but whoever loses his life for me will save it."*

To deny yourself could mean denying the dominant cultural values of individualism and comfort.

Have you been indifferent to the last great command of Jesus to His Church because it is too uncomfortable? The way to ignite your passion for the values of the kingdom is to surrender some of your comforts and wade into disciple-making Christianity.

It will cost you, but it won't be as much as it cost other disciple-makers. The Jesus Family was founded in 1921. It was a Chinese Christian community that had a vision to take the gospel from China to Jerusalem multiplying disciple-makers along the way. The group multiplied in twenty years into 100 mobile communities representing 20,000 believers. The movement was ultimately crushed because of the brutal persecution of the Communists. The Jesus Family had a simple value statement of five words. Here it is: "sacrifice, abandonment, poverty, suffering and death."[3]

In our comfortable culture you probably will never pay such a high price for being a disciple-maker. If you are going to be a disciple-maker, however, you will pay the price of one of those five words: "sacrifice." Always value the kingdom of God even when you have to surrender your Western comforts and individualism.

The Barrier of Insecurity

There is another thing that can keep a believer as a spectator instead of a disciple-maker. It is not that they don't know how to make disciples or they don't want to. It is that they can't. Either because of deep wounds, secret sins or addictions these believers do not want to be vulnerable. It's not ignorance or discomfort. Insecurity is the reason they are not becoming a disciple-maker.

This insecurity may be due to emotional pain or sin in their lives. If this insecurity is not surrendered it has the power to keep people paralyzed so that they never enter into the calling of Jesus to make disciples.

Maybe you have been hurt emotionally or you struggle with a sin, and you fear getting too close to people because of these issues. Let me say clearly. Your healing is in giving and receiving ministry with a group of disciples. The Great Commission is not only a command to be obeyed but an invitation for your healing. You are joining with people to encourage each other. Don't let the enemy deceive you into thinking that you can't afford to give yourself to a group of disciples.

John Wesley knew that full deliverance for believers comes through this relational life of disciples. He declared, "The devil himself desires nothing more than this, that the people of any place should be half-awakened and then left to themselves to fall asleep again. Therefore, I determined by the grace of God not to strike one stroke in any place where I cannot follow the blow."[4] That means if you are not giving yourself to disciple-making Christianity, you are left to yourself. You are not following the blow and the devil is keeping you in your stupor of misery. Sin, wounds and hurts are not excuses to keep from being a disciple-maker. They are the very reason you should enter into disciple-making Christianity.

A Journey Statement

There is a cost to being a disciple-maker and now is the time to pay it. James Rutz said, "It is time to end our 1700-year experiment in spectator Christianity."[5] The end of spectator Christianity will not come when your church sets a mission statement to be fulfilled in five years. The end will come when each of us starts the journey. Disciple-making is not a brief sortie in a jet fighter. It is your life-long expedition on the high seas of relational Christianity. There is a cost but there are also wonderful dividends. In your going, make disciples!

Notes

1. "Sacrificial Living," in *Equipping the Saints*, vol. 7, no. 2 (1993).
2. Brother Yun with Paul Hathaway, *The Heavenly Man* (London: Monarch Books, 2002), p. 26.
3. Ibid., p. 279.
4. Neil Cole, *Cultivating a Life for God* (St Charles: Church Smart Resource, 1999), p. 83.
5. James H. Rutz, *The Open Church* (Auburn: The Seed Sowers, 1992), p. 145.

We hope you enjoyed reading this Sovereign World book.
For more details of other Sovereign books
and new releases see our website:

www.sovereignworld.com

You can also join us on Facebook and Twitter.
To promote this title kindly consider writing
a review on our Facebook page or for posting
to an online retailer.

If you would like to help us send a copy of this
book and many other titles to needy pastors in
developing countries, please write for further
information or send your gift to:

Sovereign World Trust
PO Box 777, Tonbridge, Kent, TN11 0ZS
United Kingdom

www.sovereignworldtrust.org.uk

The Sovereign World Trust is a registered charity.